A Certain Slant of Light: The Contemporary American Landscape

A Certain Slant of Light:

The Contemporary American Landscape

By Naomi Vine with an Essay by Peter Bacon Hales

The Dayton Art Institute

This exhibition and the accompanying publication are made possible by a generous grant from The Mead Corporation Foundation.

Library of Congress Number 88-72150
ISBN 0-937809-04-7

Publication coordinated and edited by Terry A. Neff,
T.A. Neff Associates, Chicago
Designed by Michael Glass Design, Inc., Chicago
Typeset by Craftsman Type/Schooley Graphics, Dayton, Ohio
1,500 copies were printed on Mead 100 lb. Signature Dull Text
by Meridian Printing, East Greenwich, Rhode Island

Front cover: Mark Innerst, *View of Algiers from New Orleans* (detail), 1985 (cat. no. 32)

Back cover: April Gornik, *The Sea at Night* (detail), 1987 (cat. no. 28)

Contents

Foreword

The history of art in America is almost too brief for there to be full circles. Since American art really became "American" only around the middle of the nineteenth century, and considering the vigorous reactions of early twentieth-century artists to this academic romanticism, it would seem as if there should be years to go before something as traditional as landscape painting could reappear as a major force in serious contemporary art. And yet, the landscape has reappeared.

While it is true that landscape painting has never entirely disappeared, much of it since the end of the last century has tried harder to maintain a romantic view of the past than it has to raise issues of the present. But, a "contemporary" art that does not truly reflect its own time is more romantic and less relevant to its time than was the art of the past that it imitates. As subject matter, landscape was left behind as the avant-garde moved from pastoral scenes to urban views and then to abstraction.

Now, with only a decade remaining before the close of this century, landscape has returned as a legitimate concern of the serious contemporary artist. This is not to say that galleries and museums will once again be filled with the vistas of the wilderness that Frederic Edwin Church and Albert Bierstadt once showed us. The last century's artists reflected their society's awe and delight at the vastness of the American continent. Today's artists reflect wonder that it has survived at all and certainly share a concern that more attention be given to a resource that once was mistakenly perceived as endless.

Despite the evident concern for the country's natural resources, the resurgence of landscape painting cannot be seen as a protest movement. It is not even a "movement" such as tends to be produced by circles of artists that are much more closely related by age and experience than are the artists included in this exhibition. The fact that young and emerging artists such as Peter Fleps and Jeanne Dunning have arrived at conclusions and concerns so closely related to those of established artists such as Alfred Leslie and Neil Jenney suggests that we have come full circle.

"A Certain Slant of Light" is not about landscape as an oddity; nor is it about nostalgia. This is an exhibition of work by artists who have moved their vision from the increasingly internalized and introspective focus of the abstract mainstream back to the external, object-oriented horizons of their predecessors. The conclusions reached by our audiences may be very different from those of the throngs who waited in line to view Frederic Church's huge canvases through opera glasses. They should be. But the process of seeing the land through the eyes of a trained observer is the same and its return is welcome. For making possible this exhibition and its accompanying publication, I would like to extend my deepest appreciation to our former Chief Curator and Director of Programs Naomi Vine who organized the show and contributed a very fine essay to this book, and to The Mead Corporation Foundation, for enabling us to bring together and present these works and ideas.

Bruce H. Evans
Director

Lenders to the Exhibition

American Express Travel Related Services Company, Inc.
Barry and Gail Berkus
Blum Helman Gallery, New York
Robert Blumenthal
Francis and John Bowes
The Brooklyn Museum
California State University Art Museum, Long Beach
Robert and Honey Dootson
Michael Egan
The Equitable Real Estate
Feature, New York
Mr. and Mrs. Klaus Groenke
Mr. and Mrs. Graham Gund
Mr. and Mrs. William J. Hokin
Tricia Joyce
Mr. and Mrs. Franklin D. Konigsberg
Emily Fisher Landau
Curt Marcus Gallery, New York
Steve Martin
Mr. and Mrs. Frederick Mayer
Montgomery Museum of Fine Arts, Alabama
Mr. and Mrs. Lewis Nerman
Neuberger Museum, State University of New York at Purchase
Oil & Steel Gallery, Long Island City, New York
Phyllis Kind Galleries, New York and Chicago
The Prudential
William and Christine Robb
John and Patricia Roche
Rose Art Museum, Brandeis University, Waltham, Massachusetts
Jack Shainman Gallery, New York
The Shearson Lehman Hutton Collection
Dr. and Mrs. Robert W. Stokes
Edward Thorp Gallery, New York
Mr. and Mrs. Richard Watson
Zolla/Lieberman Gallery, Chicago
and other private collections

Introduction and Acknowledgments

Natural settings have been important components of European paintings at least since the Renaissance, but the landscape itself traditionally has not been regarded as a significant subject for works of art on the continent. The influential French Academy ranked landscape painting at the lower end of its hierarchy, along with still life and genre scenes, as one of the more superficial subjects an artist could paint. With a few exceptions, the history of European art and criticism has not treated scenes of the natural world as if they were capable of conveying serious moral truth or social values.

American art history, however, tells a different story. In this country, landscape painting is a revered tradition that embodies the fears, hopes, beliefs, and ideals of the American people. During the nineteenth century, the expansive bounty of the new continent pervaded the thinking of American politicians, philosophers, and poets, and its generous promise shines through the works of art produced by their countrymen. The styles and conventions for representing nature that were developed by these nineteenth-century painters and photographers have by now become firmly imbedded in the national aesthetic consciousness, and it is difficult to imagine an American landscape art that does not refer to them in some way.

At the turn of the century, Americans, like the citizens of other newly industrialized nations, began to leave the land to inhabit cities and develop new technologies which demanded ever-increasing supplies of coal and lumber; while devouring natural resources, early twentieth-century Americans lost sight of the splendid wilderness, and the landscape nearly disappeared from American art and thought. During the 1960s, however, widespread ecological concern began to surface as business and industry continued to take more from the environment than natural cycles could replace. Since 1980 this concern has burgeoned into full awareness of the fragility and vulnerability of nature, and the landscape has reappeared in contemporary works of art. Artists now offer a more limited, anxious view of nature, which draws ironically as well as respectfully on the conventions of nineteenth-century painting, but still manages to present a sublime vision of the American land. This present exhibition celebrates the power and beauty of this contemporary vision while examining the dark underside of its meanings.

An exhibition of this scope requires the professional expertise, collaboration, and hard work of numerous individuals, all of whom deserve more than appreciation as a reward for their contributions. Support for the exhibition and recognition of its significance have been gratifying, and I wish to express particular thanks to The Mead Corporation Foundation, which has once again demonstrated a rare commitment to the arts. Burnell Roberts, John Franz, and Kathy Strawn have been particularly instrumental in maintaining this commitment.

The generosity of the many collectors, artists, museums, and galleries who have participated in this exhibition has been exceptional, and I am grateful to all who loaned works of art. In addition, I want to express my appreciation to those who provided information, photographs, and technical assistance. These include in Chicago, Andree Stone at Dart Gallery, David Russick and William H. Bengtson at Phyllis Kind Gallery, Roberta Lieberman and Jan Bonavia at Zolla/Lieberman Gallery; and in New York, Peter Freeman at Blum Helman Gallery, Hudson at Feature, Kimberly Martin at Jack Shainman Gallery, Edward Thorp at Edward Thorp Gallery, Gordon VeneKlasen at Curt Marcus Gallery, Stephen Szezepanek at Lorence-Monk Gallery, and Richard Bellamy at Oil & Steel Gallery. Without their help this project could never have been undertaken.

Members of The Dayton Art Institute staff have been indispensable to the success of this exhibition. Ruth Spencer assisted with research, manuscript preparation, and coordination of the publication; her gracious humor has benefited everyone working on this project. Dominique Vasseur and Jean Mazzarella have tended with expert care to the countless details involved in transporting and handling the works of art. Suzanne Gourlie and Mary Campbell-Zopf served on a task force that provided valuable assistance in planning and evaluating each aspect of the exhibition, the catalogue, and all adjunct programming. Michael Asplan and Eileen Carr have worked tirelessly, with enthusiasm and intelligence, to promote the activities surrounding this exhibition. Particular thanks are due to the museum's preparators and crew, under the supervision of Gerald Boehner, for the skillful execution of a complex installation; in this process Richard Boehner and Pat Murphy have demonstrated unusual visual acuity and true dedication to excellence in the practice of their craft. Sue Walsh and

Clarence Kelley have believed in the importance of this project from the time of its inception, and I am grateful for their encouragement. Additionally, I would like to thank Bruce Evans, Marie Ferguson, and Lois Mann for their ongoing efforts in support of the DAI exhibition program.

This catalogue is also the result of a collaborative effort. Peter Hales's scholarship contributes a great deal to our understanding of the landscape tradition and its meanings. His lucid writing and convincing insights illumine history and provide continuity between the art and ideas of the past and the present. Terry Ann R. Neff has sagaciously edited and coordinated the publication of this book, which is greatly enhanced by Michael Glass's sensitive design.

My final thanks must go to the artists whose work appears here, since it is their work that first opened my eyes to the significance of landscape images. Although their message is disquieting, it is presented with an eloquent beauty that comforts the spirit.

Naomi Vine
Chief Curator and Director of Programs

Sublime Commodity: The Nineteenth-Century American Landscape

By Peter Bacon Hales

From their first moments on these shores, American settlers found the landscape dominating their thinking. Terrifying or exalting, sometimes both, the landscape filled the senses, framed the discussions, permeated the ideals, defined the fears of the men and women who had abandoned Europe for this new space.

Listen to Pilgrim leader William Bradford, describing the first days after his small band of religious dissenters strayed from temperate Virginia to November-cold Cape Cod in 1620:

> *...What could they see but a hideous and desolate wilderness, full of wild beasts and wild men? Neither could they go up to the top of Pisgah, to view from this wilderness a more goodly country to feed their hopes; for which way soever they turned their eyes (save upward to the heavens) they could have little solace or content in respect of any outward objects... the whole country, full of woods and thickets, represented a wild and savage hue.... What could not sustain them but the spirit of God & his grace?*[1]

For Bradford, this *wilderness* was terrifying in its aspect. For others it was welcome—an Eden already, or one just awaiting human tending to bring to fruition. These celebrants of the American paradise brought their image of the landscape with them from Europe—they discovered what they set out to find, even if it required the utmost energy to convert stony shores to placid beaches, hurricanes and heat waves to temperate climes. Between these two extremes—between a terrified grasp of the endless alienness stretching West from the beach-heads, and the exuberant celebrations of a rediscovered Eden, lay the uneasy conditions we may see in the earliest landscape views made on American soil.

For the artists, even more than the politicians, religious leaders, and writers, the space between European convention and American conditions must have seemed immeasurably wide. Consider a view of Savannah, Georgia, made in 1734 (fig. 1). Here the tug of artistic conventions seems artificial. How straight, how linear and orderly everything has become! How false seem the trees—until, that is, one sees the giant, surreally uniform evergreens that once actually dominated the region. Then we can begin to understand the function of those European conventions—even the vestigial medieval conventions of the limner-artist who made this view. Without them, the settlement would seem utterly overwhelmed by the endless strangeness of that forest. With them, order prevails—even if only the tentative order offered by art.

This picture contains hints of the central controversy imbedded in European confrontation with the American landscape. Was the American continent indeed "a perfect mirror of God," an Eden, perfection itself? Or was it instead a nature demanding perfection, improvement, the tending hand of man? In part, this was an issue of class as well as cultural predetermination and physical reality. Aristocratic Europeans, like the chronicler Alexis de Tocqueville, or the American Thomas Jefferson, were quick to apply eighteenth-century conventions of nature appreciation to the American landscape. Jefferson's *Notes on the State of Virginia*, written in 1780-81, reflects the aristocratic taste for landscapes—he had a chapter on "Mountains," another on "Cascades." In his text on Natural Bridge, "the most sublime of Nature's works," Jefferson set out the aesthetics of American landscape viewing:

> *It is impossible for the emotions, rising from the sublime, to be felt beyond what they are here: so beautiful an arch, so elevated, so light, and springing, as it were, up to heaven, the rapture of the Spectator is really indescribable!...The stream passing under it is... sufficient in the driest seasons to turn a grist-mill....*[2]

Jefferson's paean to scenery was that of a privileged tourist, with servants to drive the coach, beat the bushes for game, protect the master from danger. He is the unquestioned owner of Paradise—it is his inheritance and he takes pleasure in it. For him, it is a work of art in itself, to be fondled, exclaimed over, set in a special place for his guests to see.

Yet, Jefferson's last sentence reflects a different conception of ownership, one that developed increasing momentum throughout the eighteenth century. The stream below Natural Bridge might support a grist-mill, but to build one there would ruin the vista. Or would it? As Europeans became Americans, the question of what to *do* with their vast personal property became a dominant one. Was the landscape an aesthetic privilege or an economic opportunity? Could it be both, as Jefferson seemed to believe?

1. William Bradford, *Of Plymouth Plantation* (New York, 1962), pp. 59-61.

2. Thomas Jefferson, *Notes on the State of Virginia* (New York, 1972), pp. 18-25.

3. Washington Irving, *Astoria, or Anecdotes of an Enterprise Beyond the Rocky Mountains* (Norman, OK, 1968), p. 19.

4. Thomas Cole, "Essay on American Scenery" (1836), in Marshall Tymn, ed., *Thomas Cole: The Collected Essays and Prose Sketches* (St. Paul, MN, 1980), pp. 3-19, citation from pp. 3-4.

By the middle of the nineteenth century, this was no idle matter. As early as 1836, Washington Irving commented in *Astoria* that the historian of America's Edenic wilderness had best work fast: "It is the object of our task to present scenes of the rough life of the wilderness, and we are tempted to fix these few memorials of a transient state of things fast passing into oblivion," he wrote in the introduction. As the ebullient democratic expansionism of the Jacksonian era swept the continent, its promise of economic progress through exploitation of wilderness riches began to split Americans into two camps—one quick to claim its rights of ownership, the other already nostalgic for a paradise lost, it would seem, just moments before.[3]

American Romantic painter, poet, and writer Thomas Cole reflected this conflict of allegiance. An American trained in Europe, fully acculturated to the new taste in Romantic landscapes, a devout believer in European civilized ideals, he deplored the American insensitivity to the aesthetic virtues of landscape, and he was unstinting in his attempts to redirect Americans to a proper European respect—or, perhaps, to a proper respect for European taste in landscapes. His "Essay on American Scenery," originally published in the *American Monthly Magazine* in 1836, began with "a few words on the advantages of cultivating a taste for scenery," and a proclamation "against the apathy with which the beauties of external nature are regarded by the great mass, even of our refined community":

> *Rural nature is... the exhaustless mine from which the poet and the painter have brought such wondrous treasures—an unfailing fountain of intellectual enjoyment, where all may drink, and be awakened to a deeper feeling of the works of genius, and a keener perception of the beauty of our existence. For those whose days are all consumed in the low pursuits of avarice, or the gaudy frivolities of fashion, unobservant of nature's loveliness, are unconscious of the harmony of creation....*[4]

Cole *promised* democratic education at the feet of Nature, but his cry was inherently elitist and undemocratic—it came from the language of European artists and intellectuals, and it

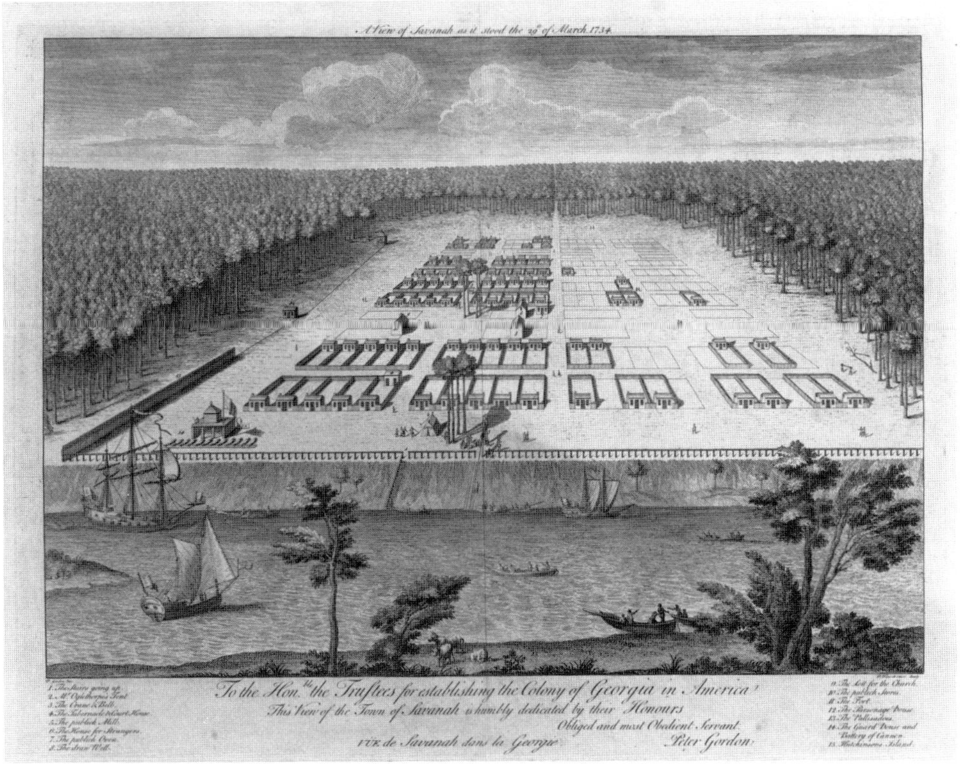

Fig. 1
Peter Gordon (American, eighteenth century)
A View of Savannah As It Stood the 29th of March, 1734,
1734
Engraving by Pierre Fourdrinier
21⅜ x 29¼ in.
Amon Carter Museum, Fort Worth, Texas

opposed the American entrepreneurial democracy of the Jacksonians. Yet, like most American Romantic artists especially, Cole was no absolutist. He hoped for some middle way between wanton destruction and elitist delectation. In his "Lecture on American Scenery," delivered before the Catskill Lyceum in 1841, Cole quoted his earlier essay almost verbatim. But he ended with a particularly topical appeal for the Catskill forest lands:

> *Yet I cannot but express my sorrow that much of the beauty of our landscapes is quickly passing away; the ravages of the axe are daily increasing, and the most noble scenes are often laid desolate with a wantonness and barbarism scarcely credible in a people who call themselves civilized.... This is a regret rather than a complaint. I know, full well, that the forests must be felled for fuel and tillage, and that roads and canals must be constructed, but I contend that beauty should be of some value among us; that where it is not necessary to destroy a tree or a grove, the hand of the woodman should be checked, and even the consideration, which alas, weighs too heavily with us, of a few paltry dollars, should be held as naught in comparison with the pure and lasting pleasure that we enjoy, or ought to enjoy, in the objects which are among the most beautiful creations of the Almighty.*[5]

Cole's declarations seemed to be about the intellectual and spiritual value of wild landscape, opposed to its economic value. And he seemed to call for a middle way. This is what historian Cecelia Tichi has called the American tradition of *environmental reform*, with its emphasis on improving wilderness, raw nature, to make it the ideal Garden of biblical lore.[6] But Cole's plan depended upon a cadre of enlightened intellectuals, writers, and artists, who could show the democratic masses the moral and spiritual values of an unexploited—or carefully exploited—American landscape. Only when they had their sensibilities awakened and their taste elevated, would the new Americans appreciate the necessity for retaining wilderness in the evolving ecology of the continent.

This was one role, perhaps the central role, that American landscape artists of the nineteenth century seem to have taken for themselves—as teachers of landscape's lessons. It suited the backgrounds of these artists. Most were children of American provincials who traveled for training to the meccas of European taste, studying in Düsseldorf, or in Rome or London. They returned to the United States full of their newly acquired tastes for morally uplifting historical subjects in the heroic Neoclassical styles. But these were antithetical to the tastes of American patrons and the needs of their culture. Rapidly there developed an alternative—a landscape art that served as the moral equivalent of European history painting, but replaced historical subjects with the American scenery that Cole and so many other Americans—the Transcendentalists, especially—trumpeted as equally full of lessons, equally capable of moving and inspiring an American public to high purposes.

But this landscape art carried with it an inherent paradox. How would it teach its lessons to a broad democratic audience, if it remained within the art market that already existed? Without museums or major public patronage systems, the majority of paintings ended up in the hands of the "democratic elite"—men like Luman Reed, a lumberman, wholesale grocer, and Jacksonian capitalist who bought heavily from Cole, Asher B. Durand, and other American artists.[7] And many of the Eastern landscape painters of the period before the Civil War confirmed the optimism and self-satisfaction of this audience. Choosing as subjects the very regions where wealthy Easterners visited, vacationed, or even lived—the Massachusetts, Maine, and Chesapeake shorelines, the Catskills—they reaffirmed the proper geography of American life.

And the style of these "Luminist" paintings suited the private patron well. Small in size, yet encompassing often vast spaces of land, the paintings of Luminists like John F. Kensett, Martin Johnson Heade, and Fitz Hugh Lane were made to seem more like windows than paintings. The picture surface was glasslike, without brush strokes; every aspect of the painting invited contemplation. Boats seemed frozen to the sea; trees did not move; the artist stopped time and halted the transitions of light, leaving the scene almost embalmed, ready for the patron's gaze whenever he or she might wish to reclaim that place and that moment.

What lessons did these paintings teach? In their emphasis on light and sky, they were designed to invoke the Transcendentalist's sense of self-eradication, in which the ego expands into the scene, becoming one with it, and hence losing itself in Nature. As art historian Barbara Novak has brilliantly pointed out, these paintings assert a new sort of sublimity, one of silence rather than noise, of contemplation rather than sensation.[8]

In making this distinction, Novak points up the American landscapists' debt to European ideals of picture-making, in particular to the conceptions of sublimity, beauty, and picturesqueness that had dominated European thinking about landscape and the landscape painting since the eighteenth century. In the major writings that delineated this model of thought about

5. Thomas Cole, "Lecture on American Scenery" (1841), in ibid., pp. 197-213, citation from pp. 210-11.

6. Cecelia Tichi, *New World, New Earth: Environmental Reform in American Literature from the Puritans through Whitman* (New Haven, CT, 1979).

7. On Luman Reed, see James T. Flexner, *That Wilder Image* (New York, 1969), pp. 87-93; on patronage generally, see also Oliver W. Larkin, *Art and Life in America* (New York, 1960), pp. 151-53.

8. Barbara Novak, *Nature and Culture* (New York, 1980), esp. pp. 18-44.

9. Edmund Burke, *A Philosophical Enquiry into the Origin of Our Ideas of the Sublime and the Beautiful* (London, 1757). The standard text on the history of the sublime as an aesthetic and philosophical concept is Samuel Monk's *The Sublime* (Ann Arbor, MI, 1960).

the art of landscape, the Enlightenment's focus on a rational orderly universe, and a human psychology to match it, generated conceptions of Nature that could account for the power and grandeur of its most extreme phenomena (mountains, waterfalls, and the like), yet provide a rational framework that could explain both the natural wonder and its effect on the viewer. Edmund Burke's immensely important essay, *A Philosophical Enquiry into the Origin of Our Ideas of the Sublime and the Beautiful*, published in 1757, set out an elaborate list of qualities that invoked the experience of awe before the grandest natural wonders, and the sense of peaceful harmoniousness that accompanied scenes of an orderly, human-tended nature.[9]

Burke's division of nature, however, soon lost its Enlightenment rationality—first at the hands of Kant, who declared the sublime to be a purely psychological phenomenon, and then by a host of Romantic thinkers, who focused on the emotional reaction to natural phenomena, at the same time expanding Burke's categories. These Romantic concepts quickly spread, achieving the level of magazine-wisdom for the newly empowered middle-class audience of landscape. In the process, too, what had been primarily modes of approach to the world of nature became instead categories of aesthetic response and then poetic and painterly fashions—matters of style. By the mid-nineteenth century, American painters were intimately familiar with the concepts of sublimity, beauty, and picturesqueness, with the qualities of wild extremity, pleasing irregularity, and harmonious orderliness that defined each, and with the list of techniques necessary to awaken the viewer to the "proper" response.

But Americans were in an environment different than Europe, and their understanding of these terms changed to fit those altered circumstances. In the mid-century paintings of the Luminists, one rarely sees signs of the decimation of the land. Instead, the focus is on the still, hushed moment when light and land, and the evidences of human occupancy as well, enter some perfect harmony. So while the viewer is invited to lose the self in contemplation of the scene, that space is most often one in which man and nature have achieved some harmonious relation. Boats, fishermen, haystacks, cottages, wagons, farmhands: these replace the European's ruined abbey or Gothic tower. In the European precedent, by Salvator Rosa or Claude Lorraine, these ruins reminded the viewer of a past human grandeur, suggesting the cycles of civilization and the permanence of nature against which man's achievements were set. In America, a land without history, without ruins, the signs of current occupation by democratic yeomen signified human incursion into the land, but the process has benefited both man and nature. Nature has been improved, beautified, while man, the viewer not least, has come to some closer relation to the Divinity that, Americans believed, was embodied in their landscape.

The nature of time, as well, was crucial to these Luminist paintings. Lumunist painters did more than stop the immediate flow of time. They also halted "progress" (that ambiguous word), with its effects on the American land. Patrons with paintings like John F. Kensett's *The Shrewsbury River*, of 1859 (fig. 2), could find in their purchases freedom from the decimations Cole decried. In the privacy of drawing rooms and private "galleries" in their homes, owners could contemplate the scenery and find in it a confirmation of the divine mission of America to occupy and settle the continent, without seeing at the same time the destructive effects of that ideology. Instead, they saw the ideal—untouched spaces converted to picturesque playgrounds for the imagination of those who could afford to own its pleasures. These were small paintings, but the ideas they contained encompassed the dreams of a new nation.

Fig. 2
John F. Kensett (American, 1816-1872)
The Shrewsbury River, 1859
Oil on canvas
18½ x 30½ in.
The New-York Historical Society, New York

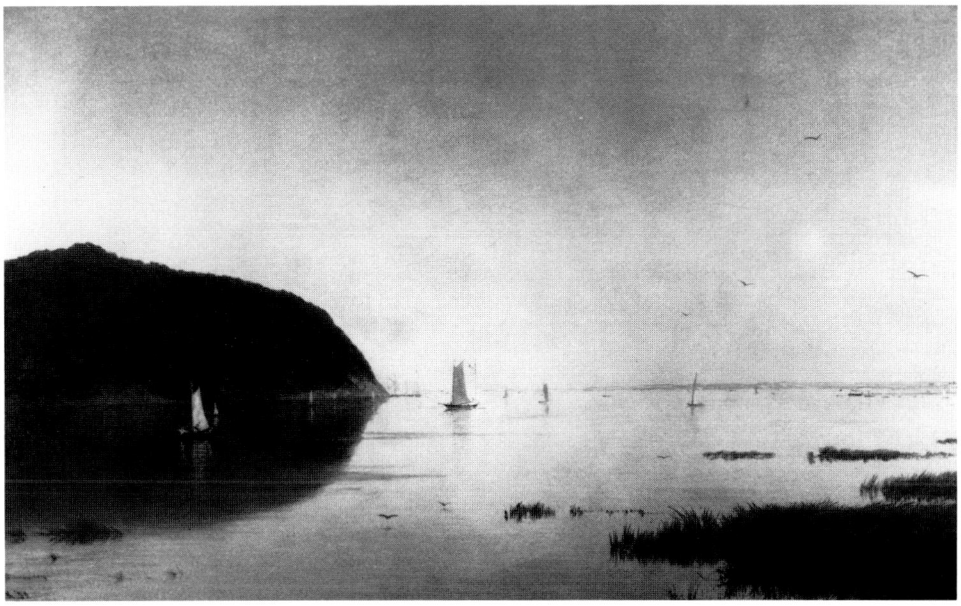

The Luminists' combination of contemplative selflessness on the part of man, reformed, harmonized wildness on the part of nature, served one moment in American landscape consciousness. But the dominant thrust of American expansion into the West and away from the settings of Luminist paintings carried American attention to a wilder and more alien landscape, even as the ideology of American settlement became more stridently exploitative and its audience more self-consciously democratic. The discovery of gold in California in 1849 instantly made American landscape consciousness continental in its sweep. And the mass exodus to the West in the decade that followed awakened Americans to a landscape of far greater extremes than previously conceived. Vast, flat plains of immense scale, requiring days and days to traverse; mountains that made the Alps seem tame, deserts of inhuman hostility: these were all phenomena previously reported, even previously painted, but now they became central to the American experience, the American self-identity.

The effect was to overwhelm Cole's suspicion of progress, his call for a well-mannered republicanism in American environmental attitudes. Instead, Americans became bound up in a wider Romantic ideology of progress, an ideology that celebrated "civilized" expansion on a global scale. For Americans, the notion that "Westward the Course of Empire Takes Its Way" (see fig. 3) acquired multiple meanings: not only did it confirm that the center of gravity had shifted from Europe to America, but it also pointed up the inevitability of expansion to the West.

One result was to generate a new American landscape art: more democratic in its ideology and its audience, more celebratory in its vision of American expansion, continental in scope and correspondingly grand in scale and subject. This was an art that would reach its peak as painting in the works of Frederic Edwin Church and Albert Bierstadt, an art in which ten-foot-wide easel paintings were inevitable, in which popular Romanticism reached its culmination.

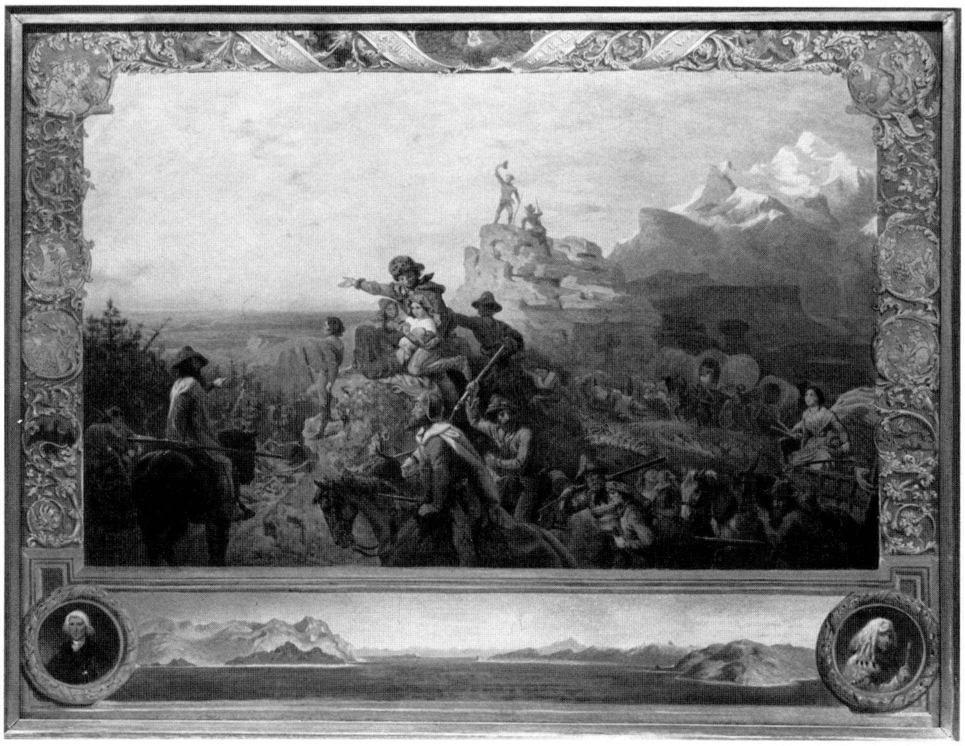

Fig. 3
Emanuel Gottlieb Leutze (German, 1816-1868)
Westward the Course of Empire Takes Its Way (Mural Study, U.S. Capitol), 1861
Oil on canvas
33¼ x 43⅜ in.
National Museum of American Art, Smithsonian Institution, Washington, D.C., Bequest of Sara Carr Upton

But if the didacticism of American landscape painting was to reach further than the individual patron, some other mechanisms for distribution had to develop, mechanisms better suited to the new conditions of American democracy. The short-lived Art-Union Movement that flourished between 1839 and 1852 served just such a purpose. It offered art-by-lottery to its patrons; selling tickets by mail, it promised for a fee of $5 the chance to win such giants of American art as Cole's four-part allegory *The Voyage of Life*, and guaranteed all would receive a large, high-quality engraving of a major American work. In 1849 nearly 19,000 subscribers provided a budget approaching $100,000. The effect significantly widened patronage of American art; it also opened distribution channels to a wide range of artists from the hinterlands beyond the major artistic centers of New York and Philadelphia. And so artists like William Sidney Mount found themselves catapulted from obscurity to fame, and their fame helped redirect American landscape painting from East to West and from stillness and beauty to a new form of wilderness aesthetic.[10]

Conservative art institutions succeeded in applying antigambling laws to exterminate the Art-Union Movement by the early 1850s, but the democratizing of American audiences continued. In 1859 Frederic Edwin Church was able to garner as much as $600 per *day* by exhibiting his *Heart of the Andes* in an elaborate setting and charging admission to visitors—a strategy Cole had tried with some success years before, with his series the *Course of Empire*. And like the artist-beneficiaries of the Art-Union Movement, Church was able to resolve the issue of democratic art while moving the locale of privileged landscape to the West and, eventually, the globe. Church's paintings of spectacular wildernesses beyond the touch of human occupation represented the extreme of a developing position concerning the American landscape and its implications. If the duality of the first half of the century lay between nature as the untouched mirror of God and nature as the raw material for human reformation, the second half of the century would see this conflict subtly transformed. Those (like Church) who produced celebrations of wilderness as symbol, now began to define their work in the context of inevitable settlement and alteration of the continent, and the mythic landscape began to divide between material exploitation and tourist exploitation.

The result was an American landscape painting with two distinct strands. One celebrated human domination of the land with a new American history painting, in which the American democratic settler replaced the traditional heroic warrior as the centerpiece of the uplifting moral lesson. Emanuel Leutze's *Westward the Course of Empire Takes Its Way* of 1863 (fig. 3), commissioned for the United States Capitol Building, was perhaps the paradigmatic example of this strain.

But of equal force was the countervailing impulse to seek out and record the most spectacular wild landscapes, finding in them justifications for American expansionism and reinforcements of the American belief in itself as a divinely inspired experiment. Here the vision of the landscape as symbol, retained from that tradition which had begun with the Puritans and culminated with the Transcendentalists, reached a new, baroque peak. Paintings such as Albert Bierstadt's *Sierra Nevada Morning* of 1870 (fig. 4) portrayed vistas of vast scale, untouched by humankind. Yet these paintings often succeeded in conflating the three dominant conceptions of landscape consumptions—beautiful, picturesque, and sublime—into one scene. Smooth, grass-covered areas in the foreground give way to a middleground of irregular, gnarled trees, broken rocky shorelines or

Fig. 4
Albert Bierstadt (German, 1830-1902)
Sierra Nevada Morning, 1870
Oil on canvas
46 x 84 in.
The Thomas Gilcrease Institute of American History and Art, Tulsa, Oklahoma

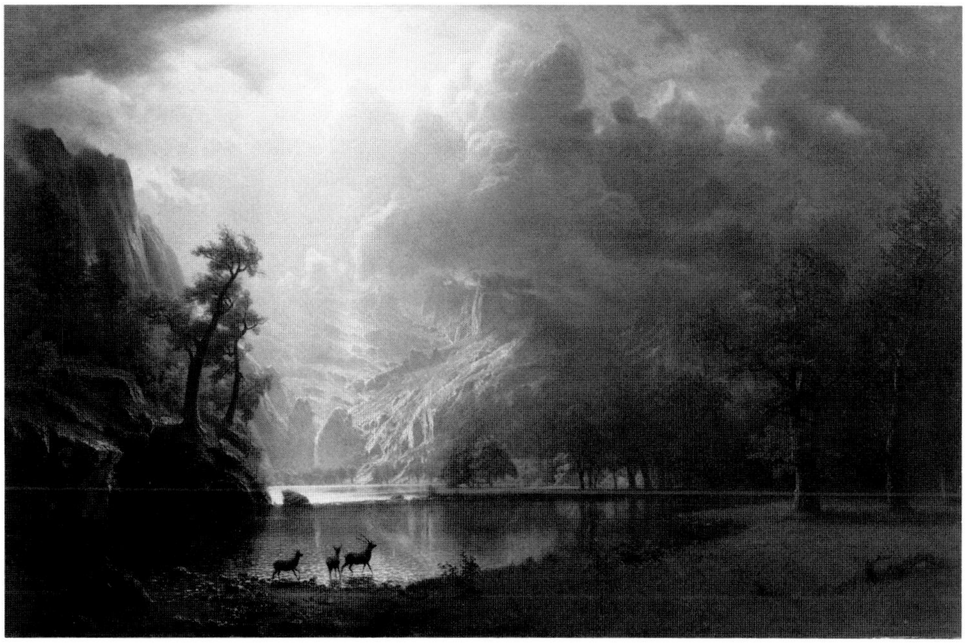

10. Perhaps the best short analysis of the importance of the Art-Union Movement is to be found in James T. Flexner's influential, three-volume *History of American Painting*, in volume three, *That Wilder Image: The Native School from Thomas Cole to Winslow Homer* (New York, 1970), pp. 87-102.

ridges, which lead the eye upward and back to the light-struck, awesome regions of atmospheric effects. The result was to contain three very different ideas of the landscape within one frame: the foreground suggested the richness and potential of the land for farming and cultivation; the middleground provided evidence of its value as scenery; the background retained the capacity of wilderness to bring the viewer in touch with God, with the Absolute. Yet what a difference between this sky and the sublime atmospheres of Heade or Kensett! Histrionic in the extreme, these spaces trumpeted divine presence to even the most casual viewer. Here was the democratic landscape art Americans had called for, declaring the harmony between visions of the land as symbol and as raw material, celebrating wilderness even as it announced the inevitable incursion of human progress.

This new stage in American landscape art carried with it an inherent paradox; every stage of wilderness celebrated by the painter became instantly no longer wild—became a tourist spot. This was particularly the case after the completion of the transcontinental railway in 1869. Seeking unspoiled wilderness, America's painters moved farther and farther afield. In 1870 three of America's greatest Eastern landscapists made a pact to travel west, in search of the new, spectacular landscapes of America's still-untransacted destiny, and seeking regions where wilderness remained for the artist to rediscover. Luminists John F. Kensett and Worthington Whittredge had each made the trip before. But for Sanford Robinson Gifford the entire experience was novel; he ended up traveling with the first great government exploration surveyor, Ferdinand Vandeveer Hayden, and his United States Geological Survey. And while Whittredge sniffed that Gifford had done no painting whatsoever in the region, in fact that artist received shocks to his sensibility that were lasting in their effects and, similar to Whittredge's already changed vision, the product of an earlier Western tour.[11]

These three exemplify one effect of resettlement and expansionism that dominated American experience during the decades just before and just after the Civil War. The turning of attention away from the East and its increasingly sequestered areas of scenery, the promises of an untransacted democratic destiny awaiting the adventurous American West of the frontier line, the ideology of exploitation implicit in this expansionism: these altered not just the subject of American landscape painting, but the messages it carried, the lessons it taught.

The most radical effects of this change occurred not with painters like Gifford, Kensett, and Whittredge, but with a new generation working in new media. Indeed, Gifford effectively passed the flame in 1870, when he painstakingly taught the Hayden Survey's photographer, William Henry Jackson, the conventions of Hudson River School landscape painting, only to find Jackson applying these conventions to an entirely different end.

Gifford returned with but one known painting to his credit. And Jackson photographed Gifford at work on it (fig. 5); it was one of hundreds of views Jackson made that season, with Gifford's help. And the resulting images swept out into the public eye, at the crest of a new wave of interest in the West, and a concurrent new wave of image reproduction technology. Jackson's pictures were themselves widely seen, as published stereographs and as government-issue portfolios. And they served as the sources for an extensive series of engravings that appeared in government survey reports for that year and others. But they also served as the originals for a number of the images made by painter Thomas Moran for an opulent, two-

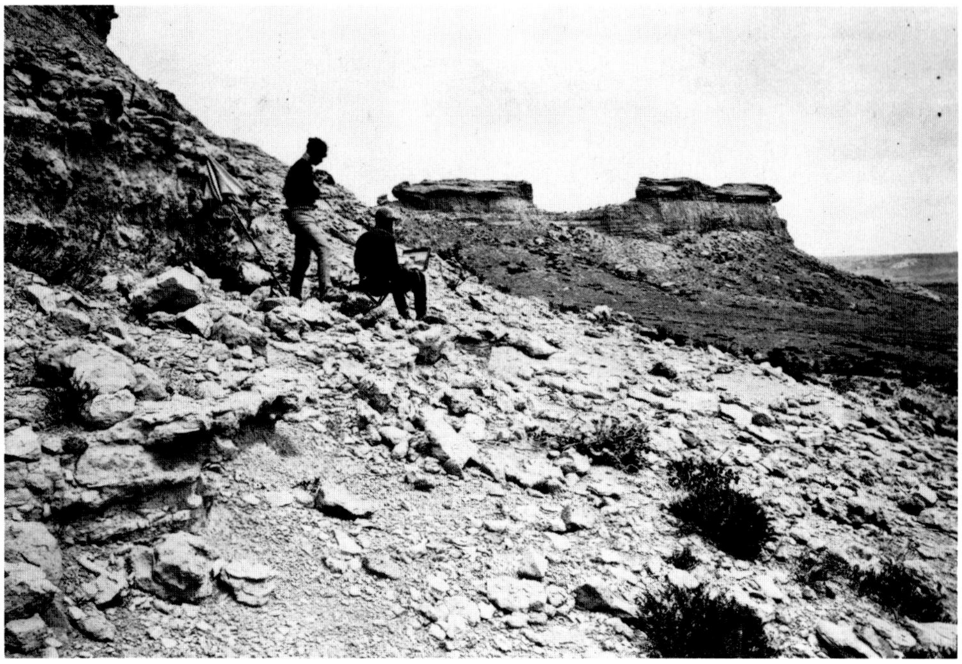

Fig. 5
William Henry Jackson (American, 1843-1942)
Castellated Rocks on the Chugwater, 1870
Photograph
6½ x 8½ in.
Photo by William Henry Jackson/United States Geological Survey
Photo Library, Denver, Colorado

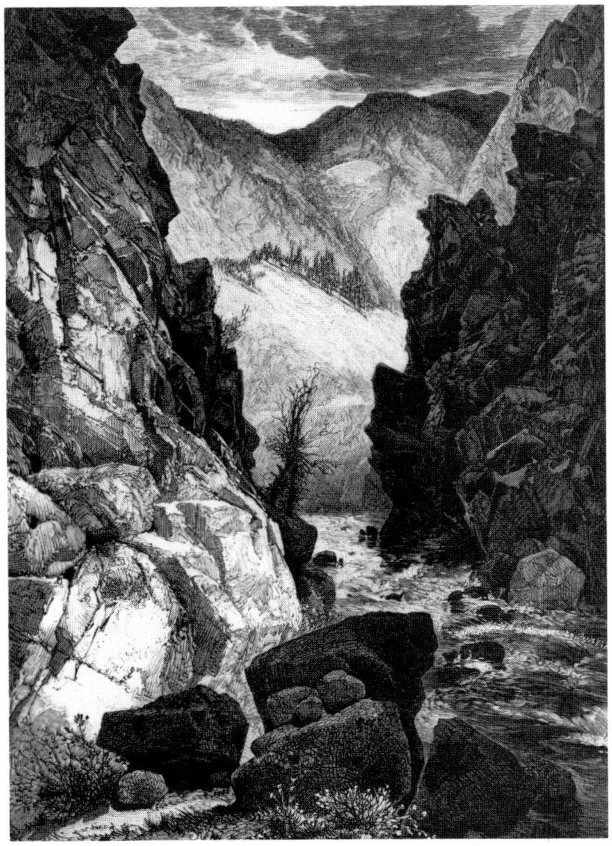

Fig. 6
Thomas Moran (American, 1837-1926)
Devil's Gate, Weber Canyon, 1869
Wood engraving
9 x 6¼ in.
Reprinted from *Picturesque America* (New York: D. Appleton & Co., 1873), vol. II, p. 183

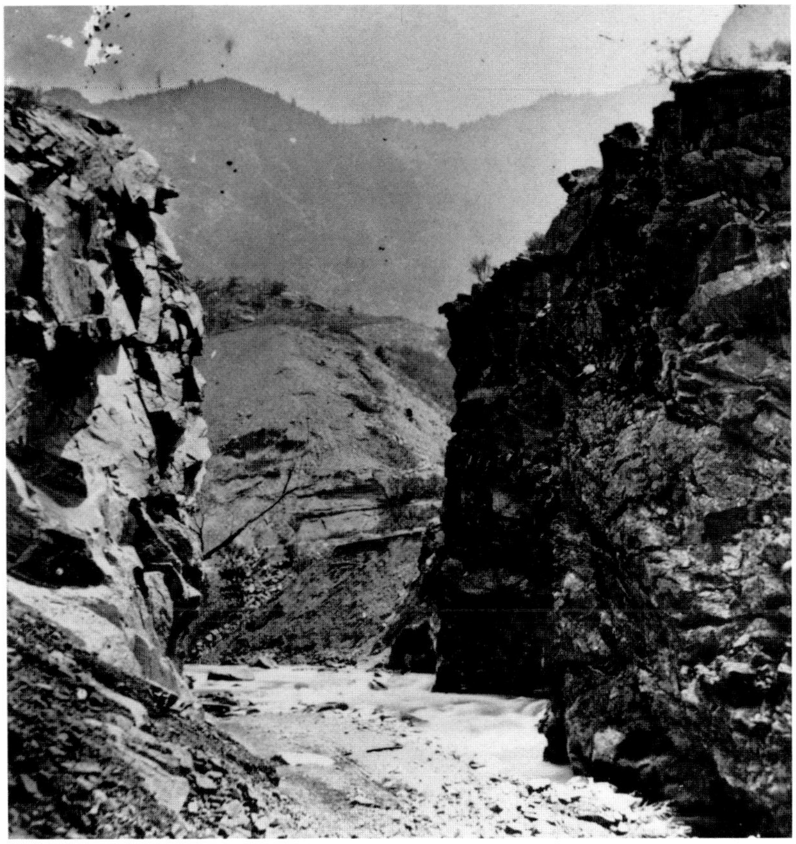

Fig. 7
William Henry Jackson (American, 1843-1942)
Devil's Gate, Weber Canyon, 1869
Photograph
10 x 8 in.
Photo by William Henry Jackson/United States Geological Survey
Photo Library, Denver, Colorado

volume book entitled *Picturesque America*. Edited by the American nature poet William Cullen Bryant and published by D. Appleton and Company, this lavish work was sold by subscription to a vast American audience. Boasting steel engravings by Kensett, Whittredge, and other eminent figures, it was also heavily illustrated with wood engravings, a significant number of them by Moran, who worked from sketches provided him by his editors, and from photographs made by Jackson and others. In both cases, the artist modified the scene, often radically, to heighten its effectiveness as illustration. Often the results took on an inflated quality, as when the painter invigorated the photographer Jackson's already hyperbolically picturesque view of the Devil's Gate at Weber Canyon in Utah (figs. 6, 7).[12]

But Moran's instincts were intelligent—he was unabashedly responding to the desires of his wide popular audience, and he provided them with a version of the landscape aesthetic that was more quickly and easily consumed as nationalist boosterism than were the more traditional works of artists like Whittredge. Moran's images were the genteel arm of the visual marketplace for American landscapes. Frances Flora Palmer's 1868 chromolithograph

11. On Whittredge, Kensett, and Gifford, see J. Gray Sweeney, "The Artist-Explorers of the American West" (University of Indiana, Bloomington, IN, Ph.D. diss., 1975; in Xerox University Microfilms, Ann Arbor, MI, Diss. no. 75-17068), pp. 277-79.

12. Information on the relationships between the photographer Jackson and painters Gifford and Moran can be found in Peter B. Hales, *William Henry Jackson and the Transformation of the American Landscape* (Philadelphia, 1988), esp. pp. 71-78, 96-106.

for Currier and Ives, *Across the Continent. "Westward the Course of Empire Takes Its Way"* (fig. 8), took Leutze's title and theme, but presented it in a far more immediate and direct fashion, as a form of visual propaganda. Palmer, who never traveled more than a hundred miles inland from New York City, was Currier and Ives's master mythologist of the Westering impulse, and this was her masterpiece. In the foreground a group of woodsmen lay bare the forests, converting them to fields. Just below, in a region still untamed by civilized man, two Indians watch the stages of Progress below—the appearance of a village, complete with school and church, which accompanies the railroad and will travel with it across the endless plains until all the open regions are settled, civilized. Immensely popular (once the most-reproduced of all Currier and Ives lithographs), *Westward* was just one of many scenes produced by the firm that celebrated Western expansionism, heroized the railroad, and rendered the Indian a creature of nostalgia.

If Palmer suggested a new model for popular artists in America, Moran represented the type of a new generation of high-style Gilded Age American landscapists. Like Bierstadt and Church, he specialized in natural scenery of the most spectacular sort. And, like them, he understood that his role was not that of documentarian but rather maker and perpetuator of central myths about American destiny. He himself said:

> *I place no value upon literal transcripts from Nature. My general scope is not realistic; all my tendencies are toward idealization.... I desired to tell truly of Nature, [but] I did not wish to realize the scene literally, but to preserve and to convey its true impression.*[13]

From 1871, when he traveled with Jackson and Hayden on the first major exploration of the Yellowstone region, until the beginning of the twentieth century, Moran combed the nation for areas of still-untouched wilderness, areas that might serve as the raw material for his "idealizations." A typical example of the result was a painting, again derived both from personal exploration and from the photographs of his friend William Henry Jackson, of the Mount of the Holy Cross in Colorado (fig. 9). Painted in 1875, this canvas began with a subject of immediate and spectacular legend, and equally

13. Moran to G.W. Sheldon, 1881, in Peter H. Hassrick, *Treasures of the Old West: Paintings and Sculpture from the Thomas Gilcrease Institute of American History and Art* (New York, 1984), p. 59.

14. Jackson had arrived late enough in the season that one radial arm of the cross had melted, requiring that it be retouched to return it to its "ideal" reality. See Hales (note 12), pp. 132-34.

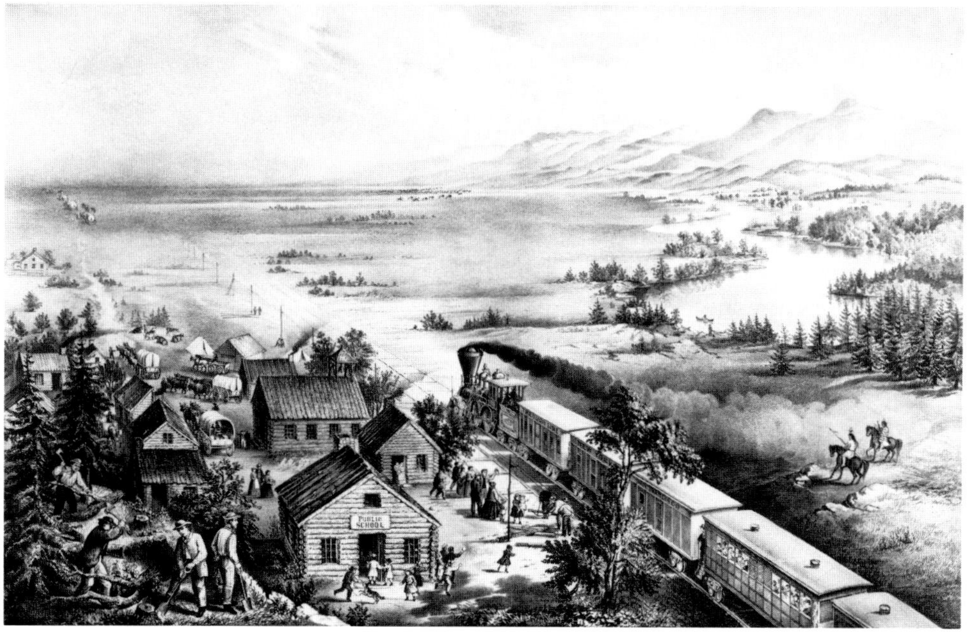

Fig. 8
Francis (Fanny) F. Palmer (American, 1812-1876)
Across the Continent. Westward the Course of Empire Takes Its Way, 1868
Chromolithograph, delineation by J. M. Ives
Library of Congress, Washington, D.C.

immediate symbolic value. What more telegraphic evidence of the doctrine of Manifest Destiny could there be than a mountain upon which God had imprinted the universal symbol of His presence? Moran's friend Jackson had understood the significance immediately, and had braved a wide variety of difficulties to bring back his image—a photograph "improved" by the addition of retouching.[14] Moran himself went out to the site in 1874, but stayed only a half-hour. He did, however, discover a picturesque stream some distance away, which afforded him the opportunity to create a proper image. The resulting composite offered the viewer a clear visual path up the winding creek, past blasted trees (long the symbols of mortality), to the emblem of eternal divinity in Nature, nestled in the sublime regions of cloud and light effects.

Moran's painting emblemized the new style that came to match the imperialism over Nature that dominated the Gilded Age. Its subject was appropriate not only for the immediate clarity of its message, but also because the scene itself was inaccessible to all but the most intrepid adventurers. Hence the painting could serve as a substitute for the tourist experience which was rapidly rendering the old roles of American landscape painting obsolete. The resulting canvas was huge—fully five feet wide, nearly seven feet high—so that the viewer's surrogate experience was spectacular. The coloring and light effects were moody, hyperbolic in the extreme. And the painting trumpeted its message through an agglomeration of symbols that were such an accepted part of American visual life as to approach cliché.

Moran's vision of the Gilded Age landscape painter as collector of the most grandiose elements of the American landscape is reflected in his choice of subjects: Mount of the Holy Cross, the geysers at Yellowstone, the Grand Canyon of the Colorado, Devil's Tower, Wyoming, and, eventually, Shoshone Falls in Idaho. But that list also reveals a larger condition of landscape in the Gilded Age—the sense in which painters of its scenes were already beginning to prepare the visual substitutes for regions quickly disappearing. In some ways this reflected Cole's vision of the Eastern landscapist as a chronicler of wilderness rapidly decimated by the hand of man. But, whereas Cole's vision had been mediated by the Luminists, who found a potential middle landscape in which man and Nature could live in harmonious symbiosis, the Gilded Age landscapists could not apply the same logic to their subjects. From Church through Bierstadt to Moran, these painters of the Western landscape had depended upon the absence of human traces—except the traces of the Indian, long considered a creature of Nature rather than a

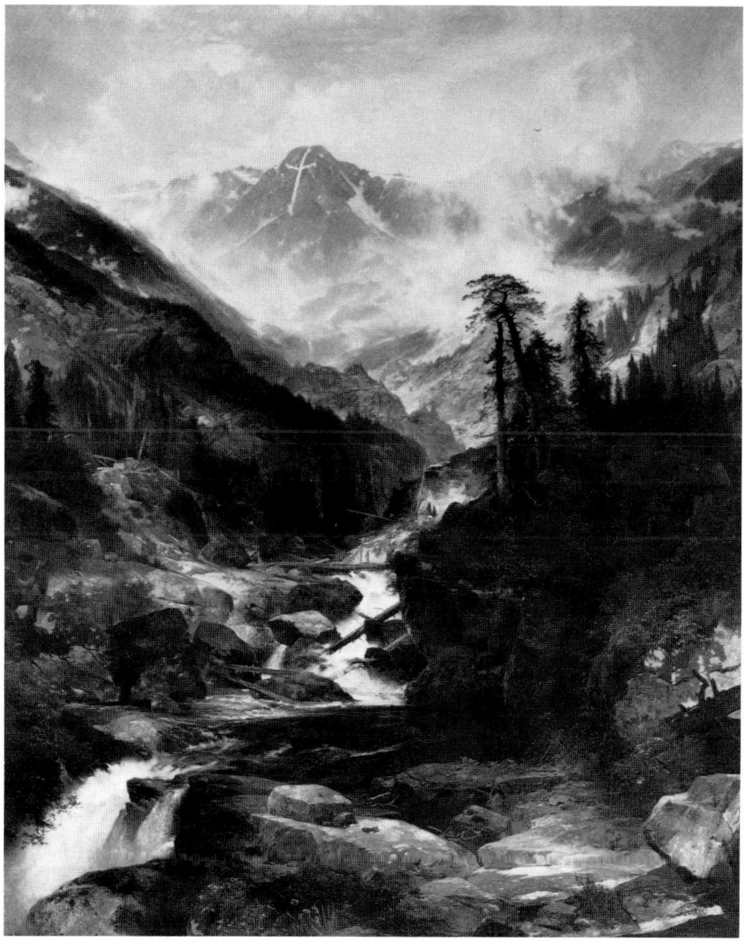

Fig. 9
Thomas Moran (American, 1837-1926)
Mountain of the Holy Cross, 1874
Oil on canvas
82¾ x 64¾ in.
Collection Mr. and Mrs. Gene Autry, Gene Autry Western Heritage Museum, Los Angeles

part of civilization. By setting wilderness in opposition to civilization, and by celebrating the contradictory myths of divine presence and human exploitability, these artists could find no easy middle path in which nature and man might live harmoniously in the baroque fastnesses of the Rockies or Yosemite. Thus they became, increasingly, irrelevant to the transformations of the American landscape, pressed aside by the new conditions of urbanization (and suburbanization), mass-production and "bonanza" farming and the tourism industry.

Or they became nostalgists for a lost presence. This was not the role Moran played, though he might well have done so. His solution was to produce works that increasingly emphasized Turneresque painterly effects, until by the end of the century, it sometimes seemed that the paintings were expressionistic abstractions rather than "idealizations" of nature. But, for others, nostalgia became the stock-in-trade. In particular, the vogue for paintings that recounted the end of the buffalo or the end of the Indian peaked in the 1890s. But already by 1889 the genteel taste establishment had concluded that such works were hackneyed. That year Albert Bierstadt completed *The Last of the Buffalo*, submitted it to the American jury for the Paris Exposition, and had it rejected. Still, the taste for nostalgia by no means diminished. Painters such as Frederic Remington and Charles Marion Russell, working at the turn of the century, found a constant and ready marketplace for their images of high-style Indians, heroic cavalrymen, and picturesque cowboys. These paintings were an amalgam of early genres—part landscape, part history painting, part genre scene. But they depended for their force on the broader synthesis of land, history, and social life that was bound up in popular imagination into the West of the imagined nineteenth century.

Indeed, the end of nineteenth-century American landscape painting might best be located in 1893. That was the year of the World's Columbian Exposition in Chicago. Nicknamed the White City, the Exposition was indeed a celebration of the idealized urban civilization, constructed for the edification of millions of visitors from all over the country. Here, landscape became subservient to cityscape, as sublimity became the property of the awesome, gigantic buildings rather than the diminished, peripheral natural setting. And even nature as commodity found itself repackaged in urban guise, as the various state agricultural exhibits vied with each other to produce more and more elaborate urban settings literally constructed of farm produce—Italianate villas made of bottled vegetables, and glassed-in classical columns filled with wheat. Everywhere the evidence pointed to a new, entirely occupied landscape, in which the few regions of wilderness were sequestered for the purpose of providing entertainment for tourists, and the vast tracts of once-sublime vistas now were the site of corporate farming, sliced into neat rectangles, their size defined by the most efficient scale for a McCormick reaper and its hired-hand operator.

The sense of an ending to the mythic American landscape, with its combination of divine presence, infinite availability, and spiritual solace, found its most telling expression in historian Frederick Jackson Turner's speech before the World's Columbian Congress. There he declared, "the frontier has gone, and with its going has closed the first period of American history."[15] In its place would come a new, global mission, in which civilization, not wilderness, became the central value, and in which American destiny lay not with the intersection between human energy and a humbling, ennobling landscape of Otherness, but with the imposition of human will on all scenes, all nations, all landscapes.

For the central painters of this later era, landscape became once again a marginalized subject, relegated to the purveyors of nostalgia, or mutated into the small pleasures of the urban garden or the public park—itself painted in the stylistic language of European Impressionism. And for those at the turn of the century who would seek some intersection of American landscape and European modernism—artists like John Marin or Marsden Hartley—painterly expressionism would dominate. In that mode, the wild freedoms of the self could spill over and reawaken the power of the land. But that creative calculus implied a loss not only to the land, but to painting as well, as the ability of the external landscape to consecrate the internal soul, once the basis for the art of the American landscape, now was reversed, and the artist drew from the internal soul the energy necessary for the heroic act of resanctifying American space in its most symbolic sense.

To artists of the late twentieth century, the ebullient optimism of a century and more ago seems endlessly far away. We are the inheritors of the bitter fruit of that era; we can see the consequences of a mythology that argues the land can never be used up, can never be damaged beyond repair, will never be destroyed. And we know as well that the cries, like Cole's, for a middle way of environmental reform, in which man and nature are each civilized by the hand of the other, have instead turned our country into a landscape of strip developments and highways, toxic waste dumps and Winnebago-filled national parks.

Isolated from the myth of Eden, we yearn for it nonetheless. Perhaps this is just the effect of

15. Frederick Jackson Turner, "The Significance of the Frontier in American History" (1893), in *The Frontier in American History* (New York, 1947), p. 1.

living on the American land. Its grandeur may be diminished, but its scale remains incredible. Its power to afford an alternative to human folly seems, for now, a chimerical hope—but its alien regions of desert and tundra, mountain and river, remain powerful pulls to our desire to move beyond ourselves.

And so the issues of the nineteenth-century landscapists remain the issues of landscapists of this Postmodern era. Sublimity, still, is a concept we must grapple with. The question of some harmony between humankind and a vast, wild nature increasingly fragile and threatened, remains central. But the light that informs the Postmodern landscapes of our time seems different, somehow—different in its look, different in its effect, different in its significance. It seems no longer the light of Creation witnessed by the artist; it is dimmer, it limns more starkly, but less well. Some force, once the agent of light, has retreated or disappeared, leaving an exhausted physics in its place. And the art this light inhabits calls a new catalogue of responses from its audience, from us: we are not confirmed in our Adamic innocence and our blessed position by these works; we must, instead, confirm our own exhaustion or muster responsibility to confront their darker messages.

A Certain Slant of Light

By Naomi Vine

Naturalism is a philosophy of observation, and of an imagination that extends the observable; all the sights and sounds of nature enter into it, and lend their directness, pungency, and coercive stress. At the same time, naturalism is an intellectual philosophy; it divines substance behind appearance, continuity behind change, law behind fortune.[1]

—George Santayana

The natural world has not been a common subject for serious works of art in the twentieth century. Instead, cityscapes, architectonic silos and factories, billboards and urban decay have preoccupied successive generations of representational painters, sculptors, and photographers who wished to portray the American landscape. Until very recently, it has been almost exclusively in these industrial subjects that American artists have discovered the "substance behind appearance," the meanings that replaced the nineteenth century's grand conception of a transcendental reality reflected in the magnificence of nature.

During the 1980s, however, many artists have turned their attention back to the hills, forests, skies, and oceans that once symbolized the American identity and the apparently inexhaustible natural resources of this land. Although scientists are only beginning to assess the damage that twentieth-century industry and technology have inflicted on the natural environment, the irony inherent in this recent thematic return is inescapable. But to describe these works themselves as ironic is to ignore their sincerity as well as their complexity. The knowing contrariety with which these artists refer to nineteenth-century aesthetic traditions is tempered by their loving attention to surfaces and details, which implies authentic concern for the subject as well as genuine commitment to earlier standards of craftsmanship.

Although each of these artists has a unique vision and independent aesthetic objective, as a group they share several formal devices that underscore mutual concerns. These devices—exaggerated frames, screened-off views, eccentric scale, and eerie light, among others—are not exclusive to landscape images in the 1980s, but they *are* essential to the meanings these particular works convey.

One of the most striking features of these landscapes is their emptiness. The natural world presented here has been depopulated, at least of human protagonists. Given the fact that today it is actually quite difficult to leave human society completely behind, this must be seen as an unnatural—or at least an unsettling—descriptive element.

Nineteenth-century landscape paintings often include figures, huts, pastures, or other picturesque evidence that the sublime wilderness in the background is being tamed and put to good use. Even those works that do not include such details indicate the openness of the land to human exploitation by their welcoming foregrounds, painted from the perspective of someone (by extension, the viewer) standing in the landscape and thereby incorporated into the scene (see fig. 1). This visual imposition of the human will onto the natural world, so consonant

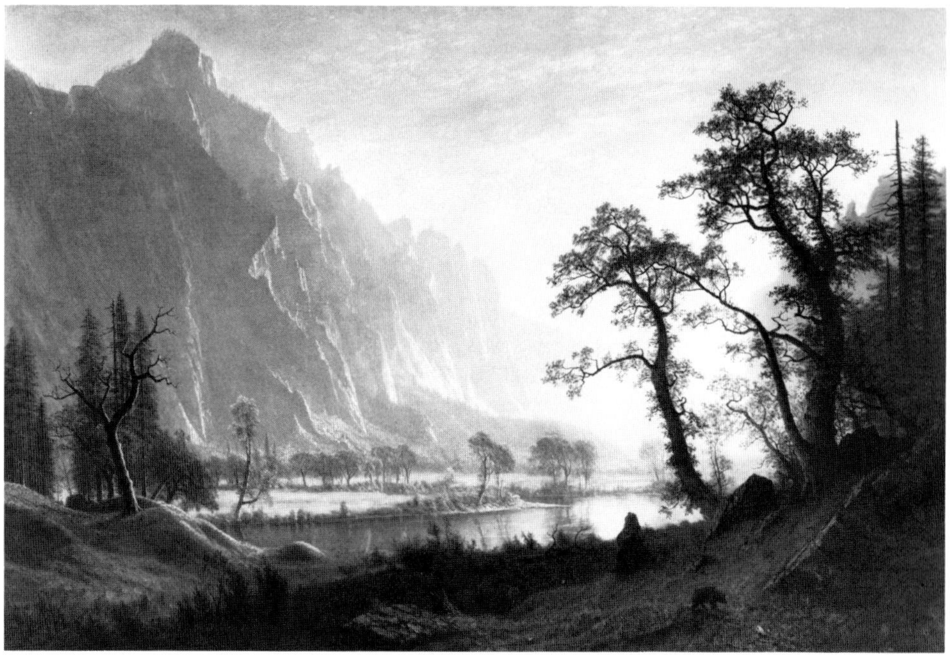

Fig. 1
Albert Bierstadt (American, 1830-1902)
Sunrise, Yosemite, c. 1870
Oil on canvas
36½ x 52⅜ in.
Amon Carter Museum, Fort Worth, Texas

with the concept of Manifest Destiny, is clearly no longer possible. Now that we know the production of antibiotics, refrigerators, and food surpluses also results in toxic waste, radon, and dangerous changes in the ozone layer, we can no longer represent ourselves comfortably integrated with nature. Indeed, our contemporary images of empty landscapes might be said to convey an apprehensive vision of the earth uninhabited, a vision that is not unthinkable in the age of AIDS and nuclear weapons.

While reflecting human frailty, the message here is not a simple restatement of transcendentalist ethics. It is difficult today to agree with Thoreau, that civilization is the cause of all corruption and moral decay, as Mary Lucier recently remarked.[2] The benefits the world has derived from modern medicine, engineering, and even the information sciences are generally regarded as good—morally as well as practically. The emptiness in these images does not attempt to cast blame; rather, it points to its condition as a potential reality.

Most of these works also present sharply cropped views or are composed so that foreground elements act as screens to block out much of the vista. The sweeping, panoramic perspectives of nineteenth-century tradition (see fig. 2) have been replaced by limited glimpses of natural splendor. This is most obvious in the truncated images of David Deutsch, Jeanne Dunning, and Neil Jenney (see cat. nos. 10-12, 13-19, 36, 37, respectively), though it is also evident in the sculpture of Tom Czarnopys and Robert Lobe, both of whom have narrowed their attention to a single tree or fragment of the forest (see cat. nos. 7-9, 42, 43, respectively). The extremely low vantage point from which Roger Brown envisioned *The Black Hills* (cat. no. 5) conceals both the sky and the surrounding environs, and Michael Zwack's elusive screens of trees are seen so close up that they do not quite come into focus (see cat. nos. 45-48). One apparent implication is that natural subjects are scarce, hemmed in on all sides by unnatural constructions. Thus, they must be isolated, framed, and brought near if they are to fill an entire field of vision. Alfred Leslie's subtle watercolors (see cat. nos. 38-41) make this point by blocking off sections of the scenery with blinding rectangles of white light; rather than signboards or movie screens, these geometric forms read as holes in the landscape, negative spaces resulting from some purposeful human endeavor.

According to recent deconstructionist thought, which has greatly influenced many contemporary American artists, there is no such thing as unmediated nature. Every human perception is rather the result of social and historical conditioning, which intervenes between the observer and the subject. In this light, the screening elements in these landscapes might stand for the "knowledge" that prevents a viewer from perceiving the truth, the whole truth, and nothing but the truth in the natural world. Truth itself has become culturally subjective, an interpretation of fact filtered through the psychology, epistemology, and history of the observer's society. This affects not only the process by which works of art are created, but also that by which they are seen; viewers are required to acknowledge collective preconceptions as they struggle to reconcile what they personally experience of the world with what they see represented in a painting or photograph.

During the nineteenth century, a picture frame functioned as a decorative addition which aided the viewer's transition between the realm depicted and the environment in which the painting appeared. As twentieth-century artists became increasingly interested in blurring the boundaries between art and life and engaging the viewer in the immediacy of the art experience, frames that emphasized edges became anachronistic. Picture frames declined in importance as painters chose to emphasize the physi-

Fig. 2
Frederic Edwin Church (American, 1826-1900)
Twilight in the Wilderness, 1860
Oil on canvas
40 x 64 in.
The Cleveland Museum of Art, Mr. and Mrs. William H. Marlatt Fund

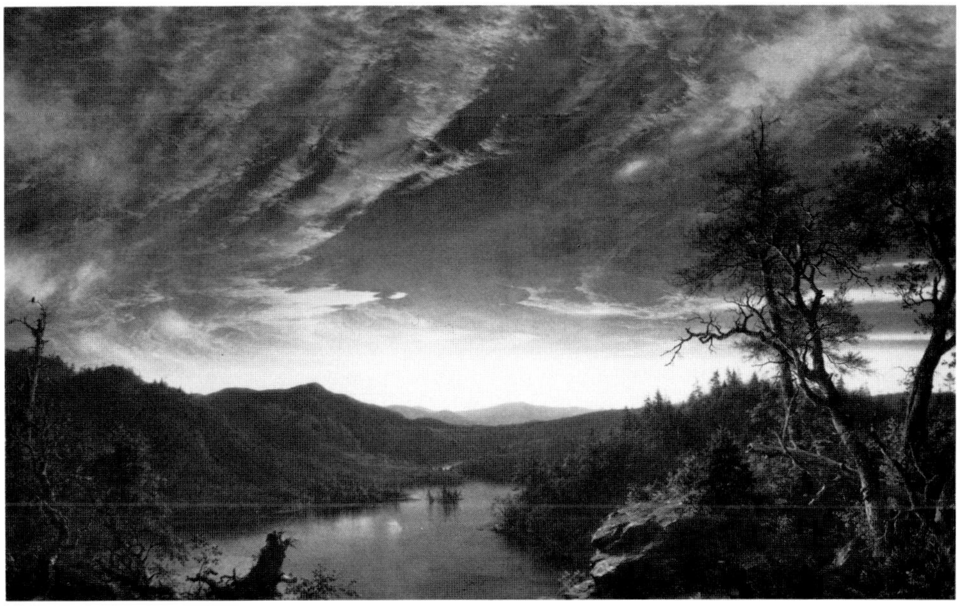

1. George Santayana, "Three Philosophical Poets," in Irving Singer, ed., *Essays in Literary Criticism of George Santayana* (New York, 1956), p. 18.

2. Mary Lucier, in Nancy Miller, "Introduction," *Wilderness: A Video Installation* (Waltham, Massachusetts: Rose Art Museum, Brandeis University, 1986).

cality of their stretchers and canvases, and created centrifugal images that implied their own extension beyond the edges of the work. If a modernist painting was framed at all, it was usually surrounded by a minimal strip of wood or metal.[3] In recent years, prominent frames have made a strong comeback, however, and now sometimes appear to be as significant as the images they contain.

Art that participates in life is often considered essentially romantic, a tendency that in the twentieth century has been associated with painterly brushwork, open compositions, and gestural surfaces.[4] But formal evidence of romantic spontaneity is conspicuously absent from these landscapes, which are carefully organized and meticulously detailed. Constructed deliberately and rationally, they require an intellectual as well as an emotional response. As works of art, they must be seen as separate from the apparent randomness of things and events in natural time and space. They are artificial constructions of the mind, not instinctual reactions. The frames that delineate the boundaries between actual and depicted space reinforce this distinction. As we approach the close of the twentieth century, the lines between art and life are being emphatically redrawn.

A simple demarcation of boundaries, however, could be achieved through far less elaborate means than have been employed in some of these frames. The proportionate scale of frame to image in the work of John Beerman, David Deutsch, Peter Fleps, and Neil Jenney, and the relative ornateness of the frames of Jeanne Dunning, Robert Helm, and Mark Innerst, both point to another order of meaning.

The prophylactic properties of picture frames are well known to anyone who has ever handled works of art. The more three-dimensional the frame, the better protected from accidental damage is the painting, drawing, or photograph. Since each of these works has an exceptionally fragile surface, this practical function should not be overlooked, although its metaphorical implications are equally important. These prominent frames function as visual barriers at least as effectively as they function as physical safeguards. The wilderness images they protect represent the land and resources that once were there for the taking. Although popular political wisdom proclaims that America is still a land of infinite opportunity, growing numbers of Americans understand that the land does not, in fact, belong to them. The patrimony has already been claimed and nearly exhausted, and the white man's destiny proved to be not as clear or providential as he believed. Whether or not the land has yielded enough to go around, there is a growing sense that what remains must be nurtured and preserved if the earth, and its inhabitants, are to survive. Viewers will no doubt understand that it is they who are figuratively being kept at a distance by the frames. Like art itself, these few remaining fragments of a once-pristine natural environment must be protected from further exploitation by human enterprise (see figs. 3, 4).

The materials from which these frames, pedestals, paintings, and sculptures have been made are also thought-provoking. A number of the artists have juxtaposed natural and artificial materials and images in disturbing ways that go beyond mere commentary on the preponderance of synthetics in the contemporary marketplace. Frames made of *faux* marble or imitation gold are seductive in their reference to precious commodities, but also in their evocation of European religious art traditions. The reverence they evince is as much for the idea of art—as a moment of sacred experience outside of time—as it is for the subjects of the works they encase. But the art experience can also be portrayed as artificial or impure, as can be seen in the appropriation of clichéd sunsets, trite seascapes, and banal forest scenes (see works by Beerman, Fleps, Innerst, Jenney, and Lucier). Robert Helms's *trompe l'oeil* manipulation of inlaid wood to duplicate the appearance of painted forms reverses the process, but ultimately has much the same effect. The venerability of nature and the sanctity of art are replaced by the power of simulation. Both art and nature in these works are buried—for safekeeping as well as for the sake of irony—beneath layers of self-conscious reproduction.

Since the subject of this simulation is nature itself, it is interesting to consider why nature is so highly valued in the broader cultural context in which these works were produced. "All natural" is part of the endless litany that advertises frozen pizza, cotton underwear, garden pesticides, and innumerable other products that never grew wild. Although "natural foods" as often as not require refrigeration, and "natural childbirth" does not eschew doctors, medication, or sophisticated monitoring devices, they are deemed more desirable than their "artificial" counterparts because they refer—if only symbolically—to an earlier, presumably unmediated, relationship between humankind and the forces of nature.

Nature has never been entirely benign, however. Drought, hurricanes, earthquakes, and tornados have played as significant a role in human history as have the gentler rain and sun that sustain the life-giving food chain. Yet, millions attempt to "return to nature" each year, seeking solace in the relative absence of civilized comforts, and renewal in identification with unintelligent matter, forces, and life forms. Fully aware

Fig. 3
TIME Magazine Cover, October 19, 1987
"The Heat Is On: How the Earth's Climate is Changing, Why the Ozone Hole is Growing"

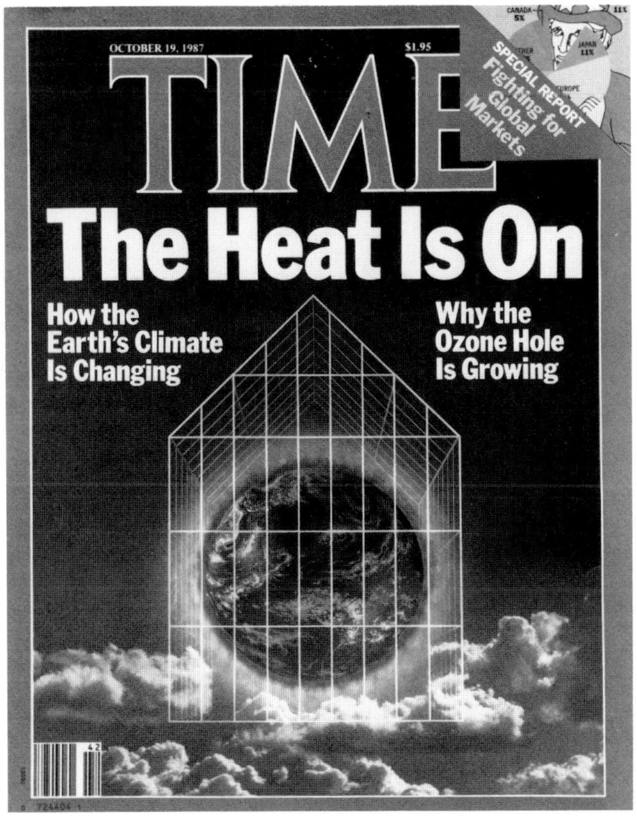

Fig. 4
TIME Magazine Cover, August 6, 1988
"Our Filthy Seas"

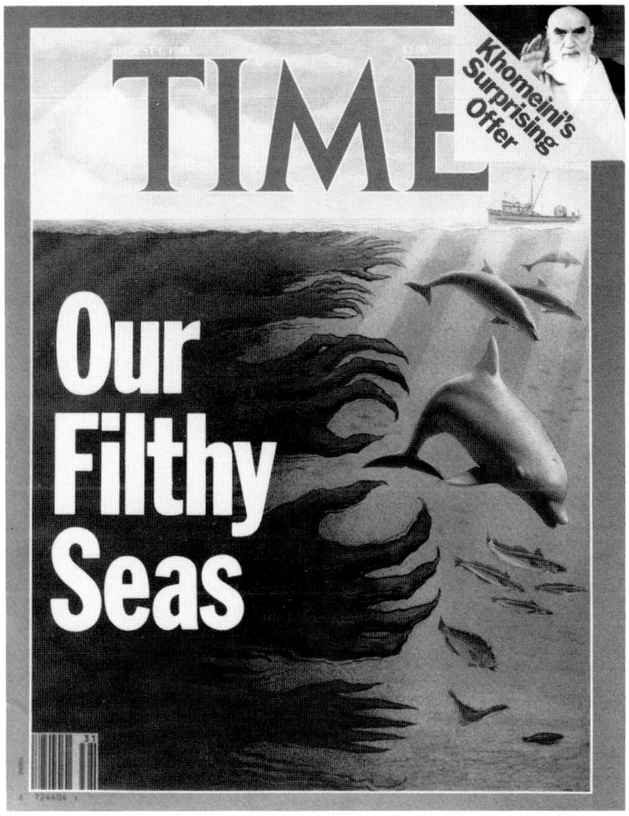

that national parks and forest preserves are no longer pure or primal, Americans nevertheless take advantage of every opportunity to fill them beyond capacity, looking perhaps for the natural signposts that Emerson believed could direct humanity to a transcendent union with the universal oneness of being.

This was precisely the strength of the nineteenth-century Luminist painters. John Baur has argued that the power of these paintings lay in "the profound identification of the artist with what he portrayed."[5] It was this submersion of the individual artist's ego in the larger natural order that resulted in the impersonal, virtually anonymous surfaces of Luminist paintings, where there is no trace of brushwork, and light is rendered through subtle and painstaking gradations of tone (see fig. 5). Artist and viewer alike were intended to lose themselves in the luminosity of these landscapes, transformed with Emerson into transparent eyeballs that beheld all and understood they were one with nature. For Emerson's nineteenth-century audience, accustomed as it was to the cultural ideal of the rugged individual, this impersonality held appeal; but twentieth-century Americans are all too familiar with anonymity. The impersonality of contemporary artwork is a chilling reflection of our modern corporate identity.

Although Emerson seemed to speak for the majority of nineteenth-century Americans, steeped as they were in heroic visions and grand intellectual systems, there was at the same time

3. For a more complete discussion of the historical role played by picture frames, see Germano Celant, "Framed: Innocence or Gilt?," *Artforum* 20, 10 (Summer 1982): 49-55. See also Richard Brettell, *The Art of the Edge: European Frames 1300-1900* (Chicago: The Art Institute of Chicago, 1986).

4. Karsten Harries, *The Meaning of Modern Art* (Evanston, Illinois, 1968), pp. 123-27.

5. John I. H. Baur, "American Luminism," *Perspectives U.S.A.* 9 (Autumn 1954): 97.

another uniquely American voice speaking of diminishment and loss rather than hope and promise. In about 1861, Emily Dickinson wrote:

> *There's a certain slant of light,*
> *Winter afternoons*
> *That oppresses, like the heft*
> *Of cathedral tunes*
>
> *Heavenly hurt it gives us*
> *We can find no scar,*
> *But internal difference,*
> *Where the meanings are*
>
> *None may teach it—any—*
> *'Tis the seal despair*
> *An imperial affliction*
> *Sent us of the air*
>
> *When it comes, the landscape listens,*
> *Shadows hold their breath*
> *When it goes 'tis like the distance*
> *On the look of death.*[6]

The light that caught Dickinson's eye was the haunting winter sunlight that comes from low on the horizon and illumines without warming. Dickinson's listening landscape is perhaps better represented by the bleak environment of Washington Allston's *Elijah in the Desert* (fig. 6) than by an idyllic Hudson River paradise. Whether Emerson and Dickinson are seen as representing parallel currents of thought or opposite ends of a gradual continuum, it is clear that today's artists no longer view nature as the embodiment of innocence and promise. While they do not limit themselves to portraying wastelands, they do, in effect, provide a revealing and cautionary illumination. Indeed, it is the light in these paintings, sculptures, and photographs that ultimately carries their warning. These works are suffused with an eerie, unnatural glow—not the simple radiance of the sun in an unpolluted sky, but an oppressive luminescence that bathes the viewer in an awareness of death and an intimation of profound culpability. By this point in the twentieth century, Emily Dickinson's introverted, life-questioning point of view—something of an anomaly in its own time—is in ascendence over Walt Whitman's extroverted, life-affirming attitude. We have changed the land and now it is changing us.

Perhaps it is because these colors are more highly keyed than those used by Fitz Hugh Lane and Martin Johnson Heade, or possibly it is the visual tension created by the exaggerated frames and sharply compressed vistas that makes the difference. But the light in these works conveys ominous curiosity rather than the "rapt, lyrical sense of awe"[7] that Baur saw in Luminism. As in the earlier movement, the light source is rarely depicted in these works, but its effects, which are visible as shadows and reflections, are often oddly inconsistent with our expectations and knowledge. Even the three-dimensional works, which utilize actual rather than depicted light, seem to absorb the rays and glow with unlikely intensity. Whether this luminosity appears radioactive (see works by Beerman, Brown, Zwack) or merely acidic (Dunning, Gornik, Jenney, Lobe), it is emblematic of the unnatural anxiety that pervades these images.

This compression and intensification of an earlier kind of vision in recent paintings must be due, at least in part, to the way these artists work. Many do not look at nature at all, but base their images on learned conventions for repre-

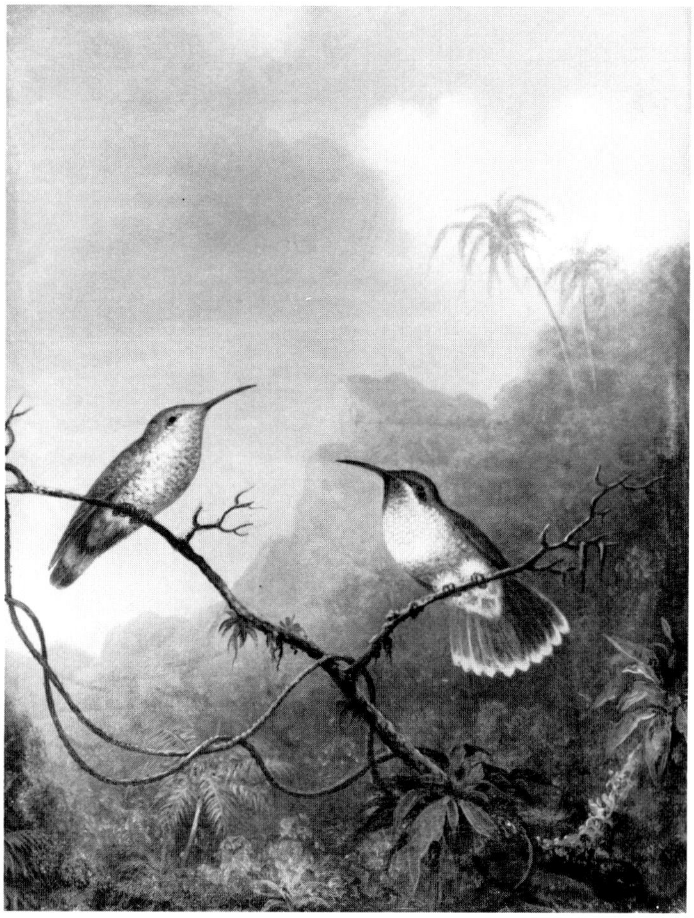

Fig. 5
Martin Johnson Heade (American, 1819-1904)
Two Hummingbirds, c. 1865/75
Oil on canvas
11⅝ x 8⅝ in.
The Brooklyn Museum, Dick S. Ramsay Fund

6. Emily Dickinson, "A Certain Slant of Light," c. 1861, in Sculley Bradley, Richmond Krume Beatty, E. Hudson Long, and George Perkins, eds., *The American Tradition in Literature*, 4th ed. (New York: Grosset and Dunlap, 1956, 1974), p. 95.

7. Bauer (note 5): 98.

8. F. Scott Fitzgerald, *The Great Gatsby* (New York, 1925, reprinted 1980), p. 182.

senting the landscape. Thus the natural world is not the true subject of many of these works, which actually picture a style or mode of representation. The innocence embodied in the original Luminist vision has been lost in the translation, but an ingenuous approach to nature would in any case no longer be appropriate or believable. By deliberately perpetuating an existing convention, today's artists can get at the landscape through one of the few remaining avenues of access, and can thus preserve what is left while pointing out what has been lost.

With several notable exceptions, nineteenth-century landscape paintings are generally modest in scale, though they represent enormous expanses of land or sea. By contrast, recent works tend to extremes of scale—both large and small—and present more limited views. As Peter Hales has pointed out (see p. 15), the window-sized paintings of a hundred years ago invited a sense of ownership, both of the land and of the work of art. The smaller contemporary works extend this idea, resembling precious, jewellike commodities that are easily purchased, pocketed, and consumed in private. The larger pieces overwhelm the viewer—not with their majesty, but simply with their size. In effect, this forces a confrontation with enormity: of the idea of nature, of the American continent, of the harm that has already been done, and of the beauty that remains.

Representations of the landscape are somewhat anachronistic in the postindustrial decade of the 1980s. Perhaps it is because nature itself is generally perceived at several removes that today's artists find it necessary to present the world through massive frames, compositional screens, distortions of scale, and filters of history and style. Their haunting images of the land offer glimpses of the beauty and strangeness that early explorers must have felt on seeing the American wilderness for the first time. At the close of *The Great Gatsby*, F. Scott Fitzgerald—through the character of Nick—attempted to envision the untouched new world and to fathom the meanings it held for Dutch sailors arriving to explore its virgin coasts:

> *For a transitory enchanted moment man must have held his breath in the presence of this continent, compelled into an aesthetic contemplation he neither understood nor desired, face to face for the last time in history with something commensurate to his capacity for wonder.*[8]

Through works of art, brief glints of the sublime are still permitted. But when the continent and its promises wither, what happens to the dream, what becomes of the wonder?

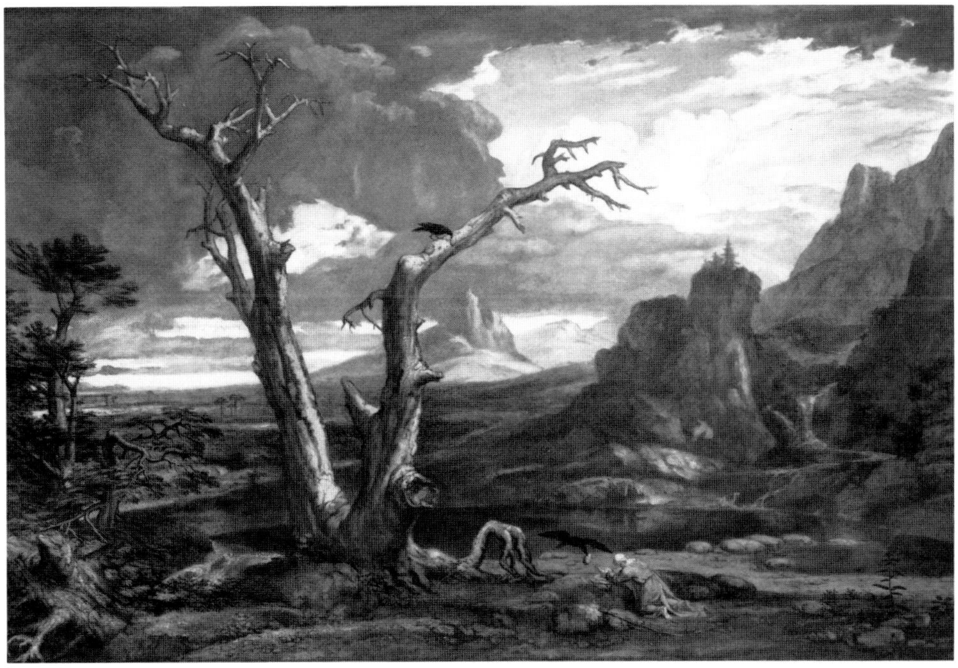

Fig. 6
Washington Allston (American, 1779-1843)
Elijah in the Desert, 1818
Casein on canvas
49 x 72½ in.
Museum of Fine Arts, Boston, Gift of Mrs. Samuel Hooper and Miss Alice Hooper

John Beerman

John Beerman's scorching color and light are derived from his nineteenth-century inspiration, the Luminist painter Fitz Hugh Lane, though transposed into a thoroughly contemporary mode. The illusionism of Beerman's hand-painted, *trompe l'oeil* marble frames is as convincing as that of his becalmed, airless outdoor spaces. Indeed, the clouds, hills, and boulders in his paintings all seem to be made of the same marble substance, and to share a molecular structure with the Plexiglas and Masonite on which the works are painted. This similarity does not result from a lack of skill, but rather from a desire to question the limits of representation and to challenge the conventions for depicting natural structures.

The glow that emanates from Beerman's paintings brings them dangerously close to the brink of banality, particularly within their potentially precious small-scale format. In each case, however, they are rescued by the artist's classical sense of form; nowhere is the simplified universality of the image allowed to degenerate into trivial detail. Each boulder Beerman paints is every boulder in human experience, though none is overly familiar. In the end, these silent images convey a sense of wonder for the permanence, solidity, and obdurate silence of nature.

The provocative titles that accompany these paintings seem at first to be baffling and gratuitous. Prolonged viewing, however, leaves the audience longing for a mediating force that might enable a meaningful relationship with the natural world. Beerman's titles suggest routes to reconciliation that are simultaneously utterly simple and impossibly difficult: *Let Us Learn to Live Swaying, Quit the False Good,* and *Suggesting the Forgotten* (cat. nos. 1-3).

Born: 1958, Greensboro, North Carolina

Education

1982 B.F.A., Rhode Island School of Design, Providence

1980 Skowhegan School of Painting and Sculpture, Maine

Fellowships and Awards

1986 Invitation to Vinalhaven Press, Maine

1984 Yaddo Fellowship

1980 Scholarships to Skowhegan School of Painting and Sculpture, Maine

Selected One-Person Exhibitions

1987 Lorence-Monk Gallery, New York

1986 Dart Gallery, Chicago

Selected Group Exhibitions

1987 Whitney Museum of American Art, Stamford, Connecticut, "The New Romantic Landscape"
Condeso-Lawler Gallery, New York, "The Vinalhaven Press, 1984-1986"

1986 Lorence-Monk Gallery, New York, "The Manor in the Landscape"
56 Bleecker Gallery, New York, "Mainly on the Plane"
Herbert H. Lehman College Art Gallery, CUNY New York, "Landscape in the Age of Anxiety"
Portland Museum of Art, Maine, "Vinalhaven Press, 1984-1986"
Lorence-Monk Gallery, New York, "Print Review, 1983-85"
The Brooklyn Museum, New York,"Public and Private: American Prints Today"
The National Academy of Design, New York, "Juried Exhibition"
Saxon-Lee Gallery, Los Angeles, "The Back Room"

1985 Lorence-Monk Gallery, New York
Mary Ryan Gallery, New York, "New Prints by Twenty Artists"
Grolier Club, New York, "Selections from the Rutgers Archives for Printmaking Studios"
Weatherspoon Art Gallery, University of North Carolina, Greensboro, "Art on Paper"

1984 Guild Hall, East Hampton, New York

1982 Rockland Center for the Arts, West Nyack, New York, "Eleven Under Thirty"

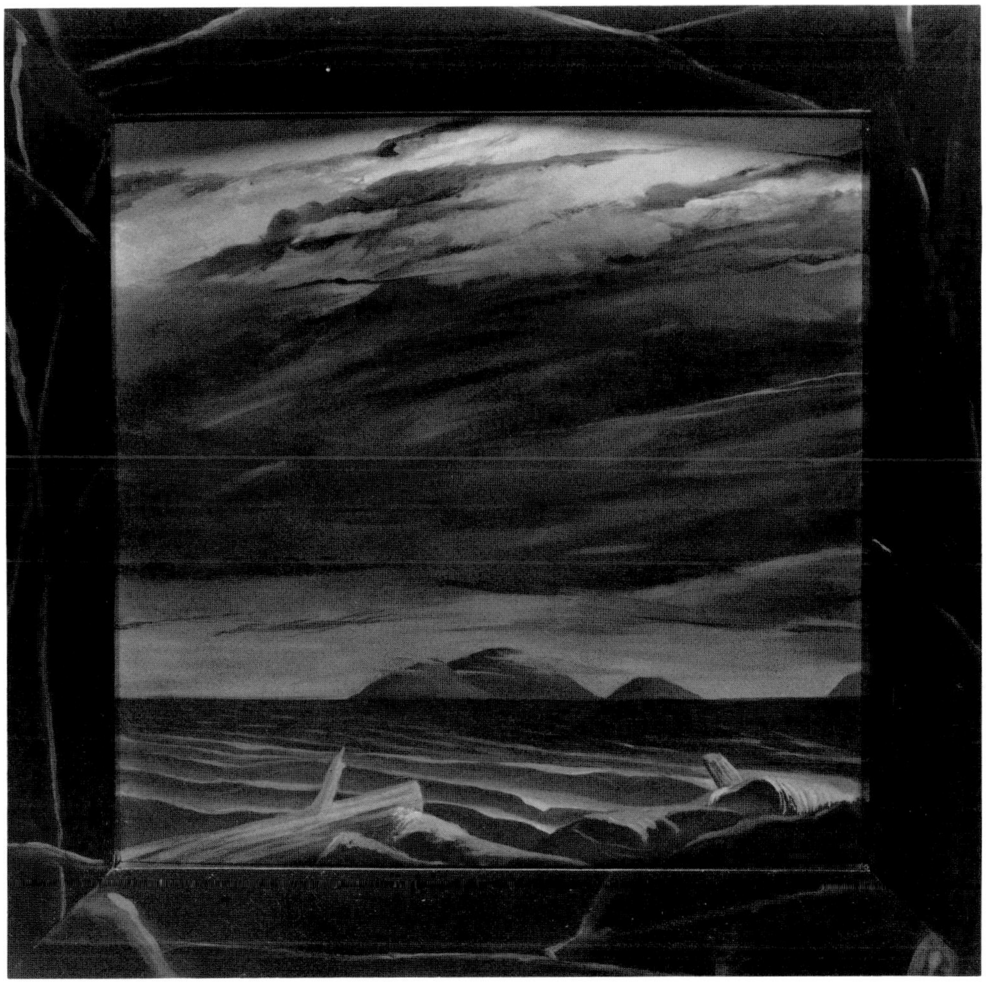

1. John Beerman, *Let Us Learn to Live Swaying*, 1986 (cat. no. 1)

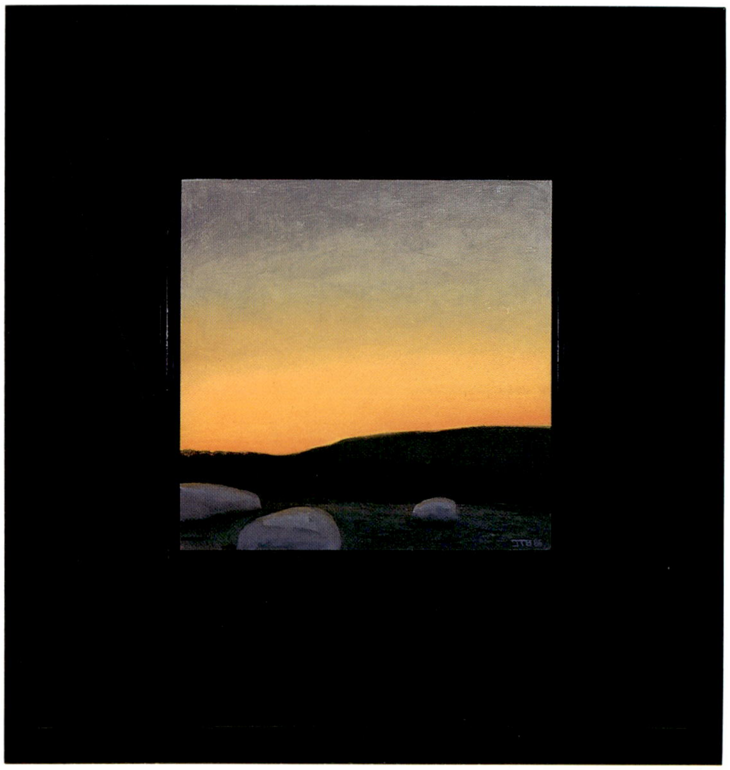

2. John Beerman, *Quit the False Good*, 1986 (cat. no. 2)

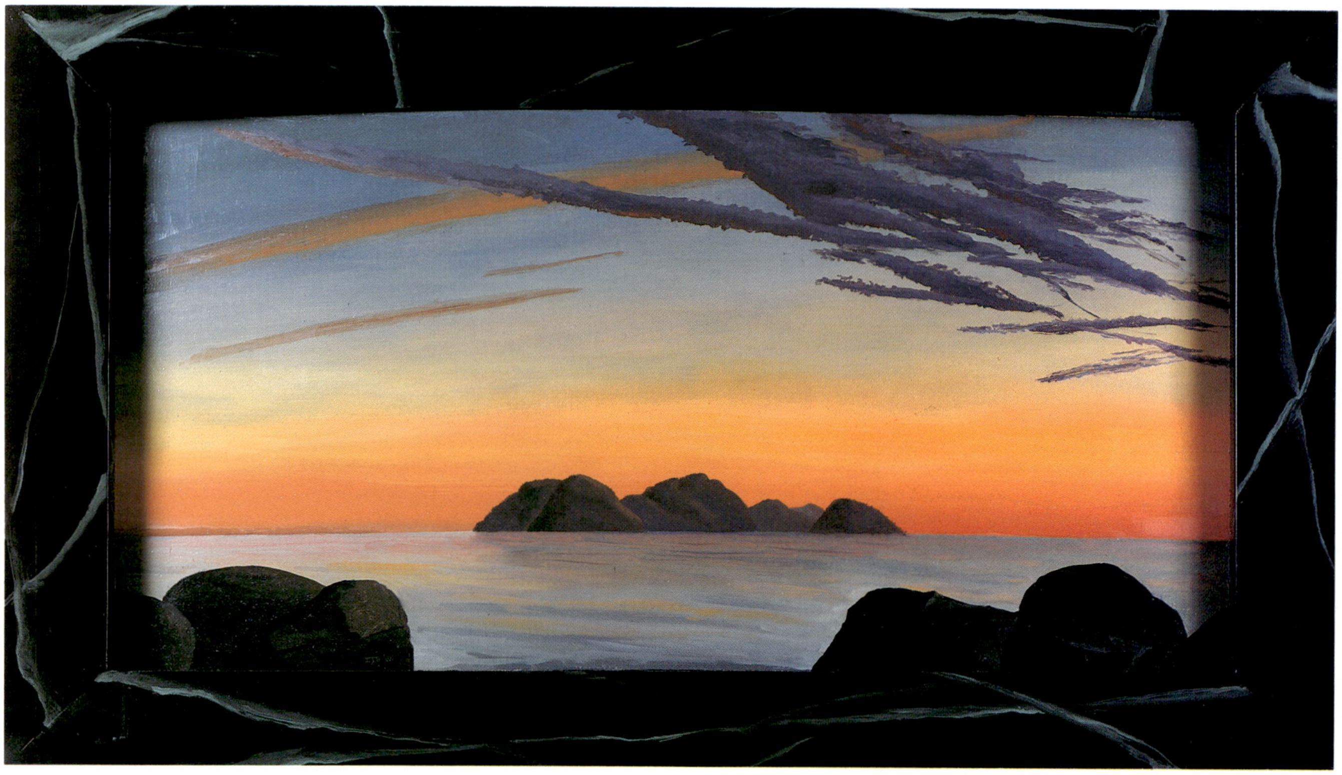

3. John Beerman, *Suggesting the Forgotten*, 1986 (cat. no. 3)

Roger Brown

Roger Brown's landscape paintings are quieter and less ironic than his humorous narrative depictions of human activity. Despite their stylized forms, there is in these works a heartfelt truth of observation similar to that found in the strong linear patterns of Japanese woodblock prints.

The key to these works seems to lie in their perspective—the unusual point of view that has been chosen in order to fill the canvas with the natural image and to exclude extraneous elements. Thus *Arctic Moon* (cat. no. 6) shows only a section of the sky, while *Celebration of the Uncultivated—A Garden of the Wild* (cat. no. 4) magnifies a tiny fragment of a field of wildflowers to fill an enormous canvas. These oddly angled views make the most familiar objects appear extremely strange, though the terrain represented is not at all hostile or forbidding. By eliminating unnatural details, Brown presents the natural world as a refuge from civilization and human intercourse, but simultaneously makes viewers aware of the formal manipulations that were necessary to this conceit. The consciousness of what is missing from these pictures underscores the poignant fragility of their subjects.

Brown's vision of the American landscape has been shaped by his numerous cross-country trips, which have provided him with both an overview of the geometric patterns formed by hills, mountains, fields, and clouds, and a deep familiarity with specific visual details. The two extremes, the universal and the particular, are so well integrated that it is tempting to see these paintings as expressions of George Santayana's view of man which explains thought and interpretation—the willful imposition of conscious order on random nature—as natural and necessary results of existence; in Santayana's system, they are seen as no less natural than digestion.

The Black Hills (cat. no. 5) was painted as a tribute to one of the artist's closest friends, an architect who had grown up in South Dakota and who died of cancer in 1984. The simple, reductive composition is sober and monumental, a fitting memorial to a modernist sensibility and a solemn commemoration of the once-expansive badlands. As in the echoing cry of the snow wolf in *Arctic Moon*, there is dignity as well as pain in the simplified landscapes Brown paints. The sense of loss is inescapable, but it is tempered by the beauty and grace of nature.

Born: 1941, Hamilton, Alabama

Education

1970 M.F.A., The School of the Art Institute of Chicago
1968 B.F.A., The School of the Art Institute of Chicago
1962-64 American Academy of Art, Chicago

Selected One-Person Exhibitions

1988 Phyllis Kind Gallery, Chicago
Asher/Faure Gallery, Los Angeles
1987-88 Hirshhorn Museum and Sculpture Garden, Washington, D.C., "Roger Brown" (traveled to La Jolla Museum of Contemporary Art, California; Lowe Art Museum, University of Miami, Coral Gables, Florida; Des Moines Art Center, Iowa)
1987 Fendrick Gallery, Washington, D.C.
Phyllis Kind Gallery, New York
1986 John Berggruen Gallery, San Francisco
Phyllis Kind Gallery, Chicago
1985 Texas Gallery, Houston
Phyllis Kind Gallery, New York
1984-85 Nexus Gallery, Atlanta, "Roger Brown: A Selected Retrospective" (traveled to University of South Florida Art Galleries, Tampa; North Carolina Museum of Art, Raleigh)
1984 Phyllis Kind Gallery, New York
1983 Asher/Faure Gallery, Los Angeles
1982 Phyllis Kind Gallery, New York
1981 Mayor Gallery, London
Phyllis Kind Gallery, New York
1980-81 Montgomery Museum of Fine Art, Alabama, "Roger Brown" (traveled to The Contemporary Arts Museum, Houston; Museum of Contemporary Art, Chicago)
1980 The Saint Louis Art Museum, "Currents"
University Art Museum, Berkeley, California, "Matrix/ Berkeley 35"
1979 Phyllis Kind Gallery, Chicago
Phyllis Kind Gallery, New York
1977 Phyllis Kind Gallery, New York
1976 Phyllis Kind Gallery, Chicago
1975 Phyllis Kind Gallery, New York
1974 Peale House, The Pennsylvania Academy of The Fine Arts, Philadelphia
Phyllis Kind Gallery, Chicago
Galerie Darthea Speyer, Paris
1973 Phyllis Kind Gallery, Chicago
1971 Phyllis Kind Gallery, Chicago

Selected Group Exhibitions

Roger Brown has participated in hundreds of group exhibitions throughout the United States and Europe since the late 1960s. These are far too numerous to list here.

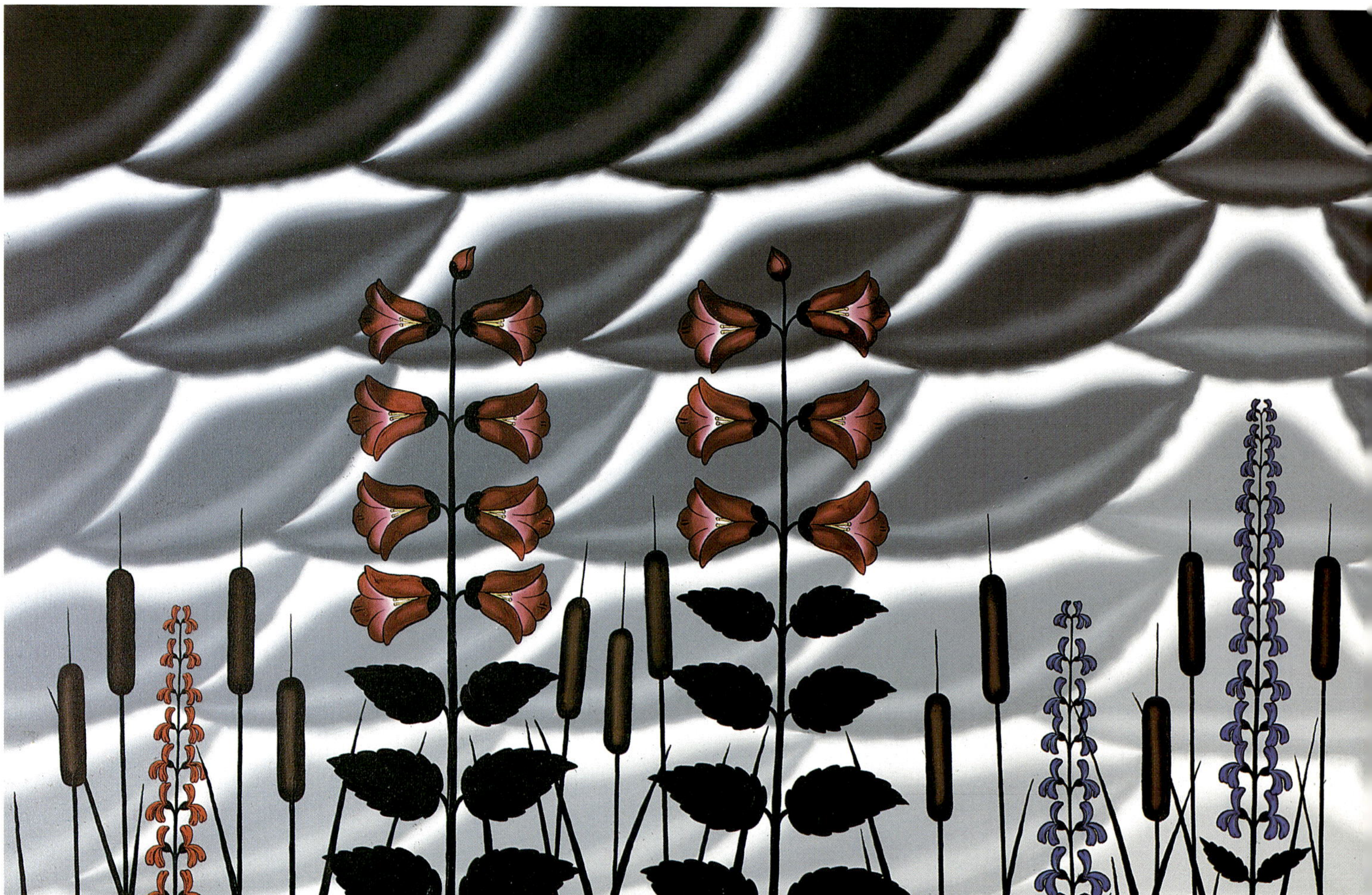

4. Roger Brown, *Celebration of the Uncultivated—A Garden of the Wild*, 1980 (cat. no. 4)

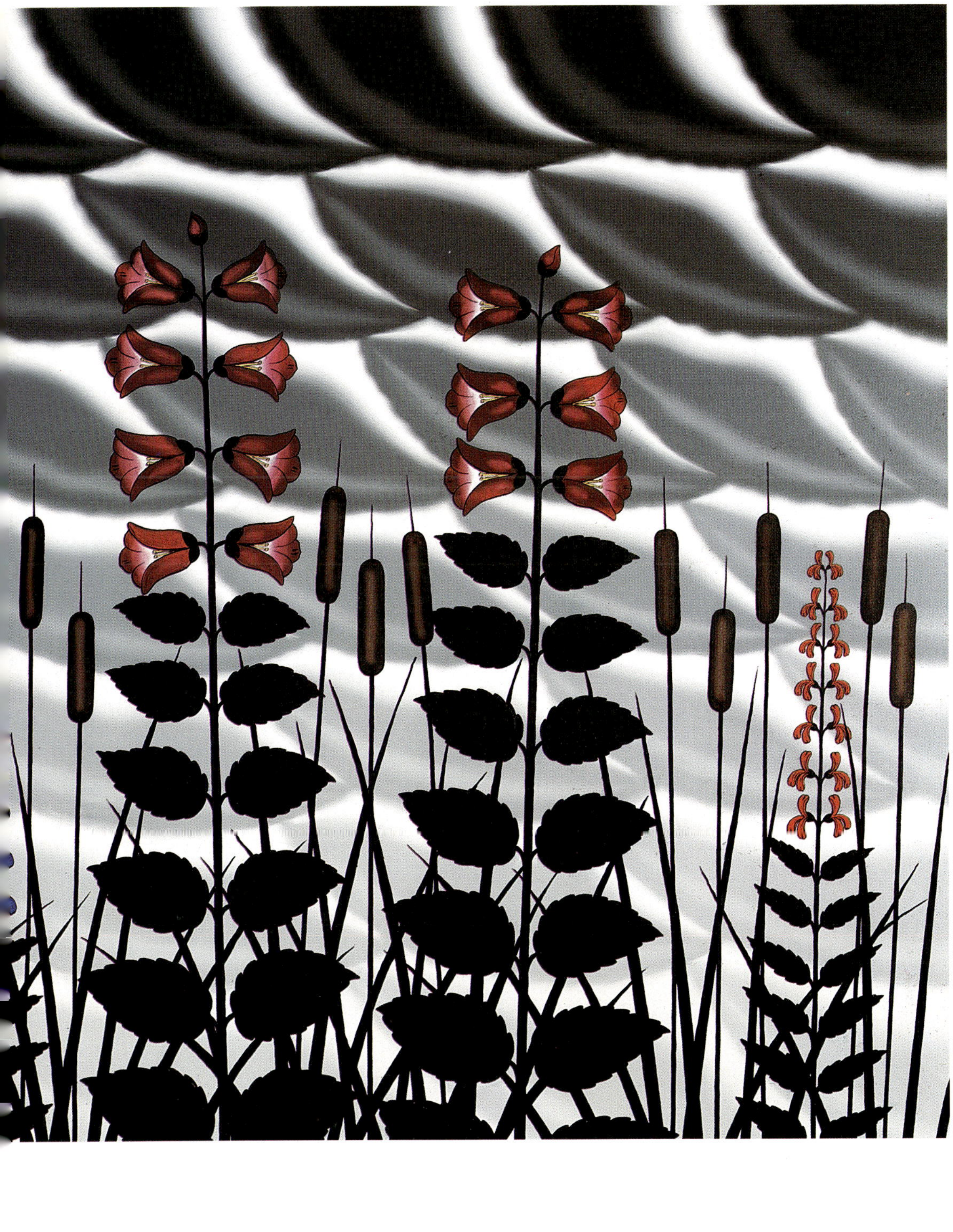

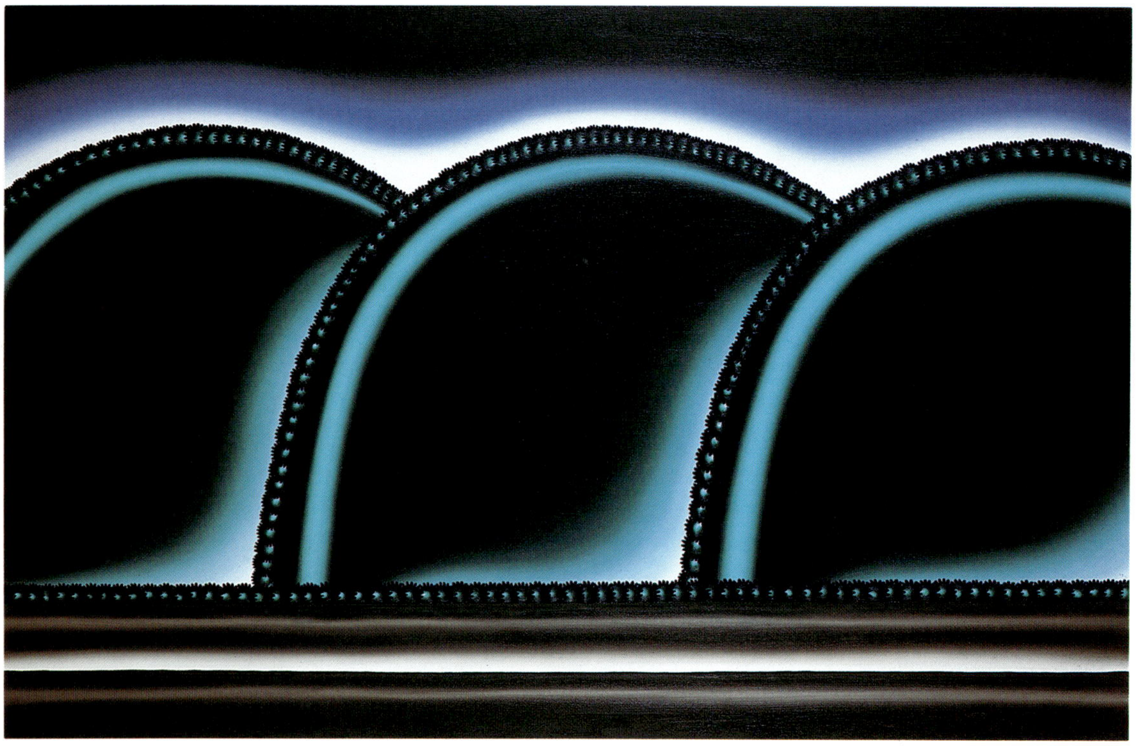

5. Roger Brown, *The Black Hills*, 1984 (cat. no. 5)

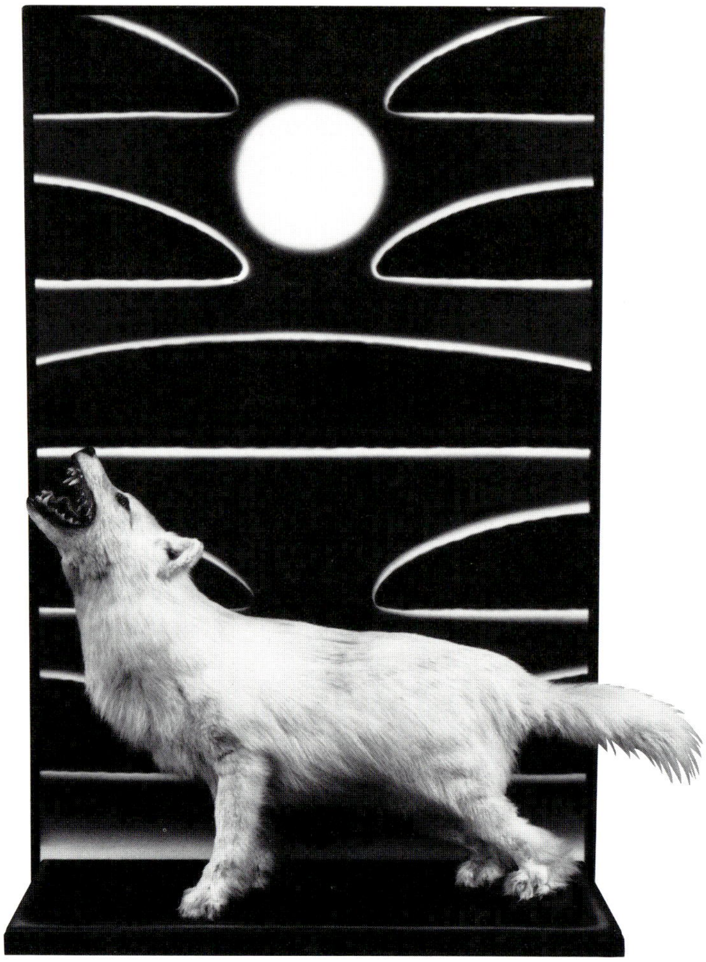

6. Roger Brown, *Arctic Moon*, 1987 (cat. no. 6)

Tom Czarnopys

Tom Czarnopys's sculpture evokes the animistic myths of antiquity in which human, animal, and plant forms become interchangeable. In this work, the spiritual relationship between the landscape and its human dependents is examined and convincingly revealed through authoritative visual metaphors that have the impact of profound truth.

The human figures in these pieces appear in various stages of coalescence with inanimate nature, thus they embody the transcendental ideal of oneness and unity. It is always somewhat disturbing to see the human form altered or disrupted, but here it is the ego or identity that seems to be suppressed. Whether the newborn is emerging from the landscape, as in *Birthing Figure* (cat. no. 8), or the fully developed adult form is in the process of reintegrating itself with the natural world, as in *Somnambulist* (cat. no. 7), no individualism or unique personality asserts itself. This is true of the artist as well as the figures he creates; like the Luminist painters, Czarnopys hides all traces of his own touch in a painstaking technique which produces surfaces so naturalistic that they appear not to be handmade at all.

Czarnopys developed his method and imagery out of an interest in camouflage, which attempts to minimize the boundaries between hunter and hunted. His sculpted forms have an even more far-reaching goal: to eliminate the boundaries between culture and nature. The convincing synthesis of forms which embody rational thought and prerational existence posits the possibility of a conjunction between the conscious intellect, which needs and creates civilization, and the unconscious mind, which craves a reunion with inanimate nature.

Born: 1957, Grand Rapids, Michigan

Education

1982 B.F.A., The School of the Art Institute of Chicago

Selected One-Person Exhibitions

1987 Grand Rapids Art Museum, Michigan, "Nature of Passion, Passion of Nature" (traveled to Contemporary Arts Center, Cincinnati, Ohio)

Selected Group Exhibitions

1987 Zolla/Lieberman Gallery, Chicago, "New Glory in Sculpture"

1986 Indianapolis Museum of Art, Indiana, "Painting and Sculpture Today"
Dart Gallery, Chicago

1985 Contemporary Arts Center, Cincinnati, Ohio, "Body and Soul: Aspects of Recent Figurative Sculpture"
Museum of Contemporary Art, Chicago, "Selections from the Permanent Collection: The Figure in Chicago Art"
Dart Gallery, Inc., Chicago, "A Chicago Souvenir"
Randolph Street Gallery, Chicago, "Installations"

1984 ARC Gallery, Chicago, "Fall 1984-UN-Scene"

1983 The School of the Art Institute of Chicago, "Aspects of Landscape"

1982 The School of the Art Institute of Chicago, "The School Show"

1981 Bendigo College, Victoria Falls, Australia, "Group Drawing Show"

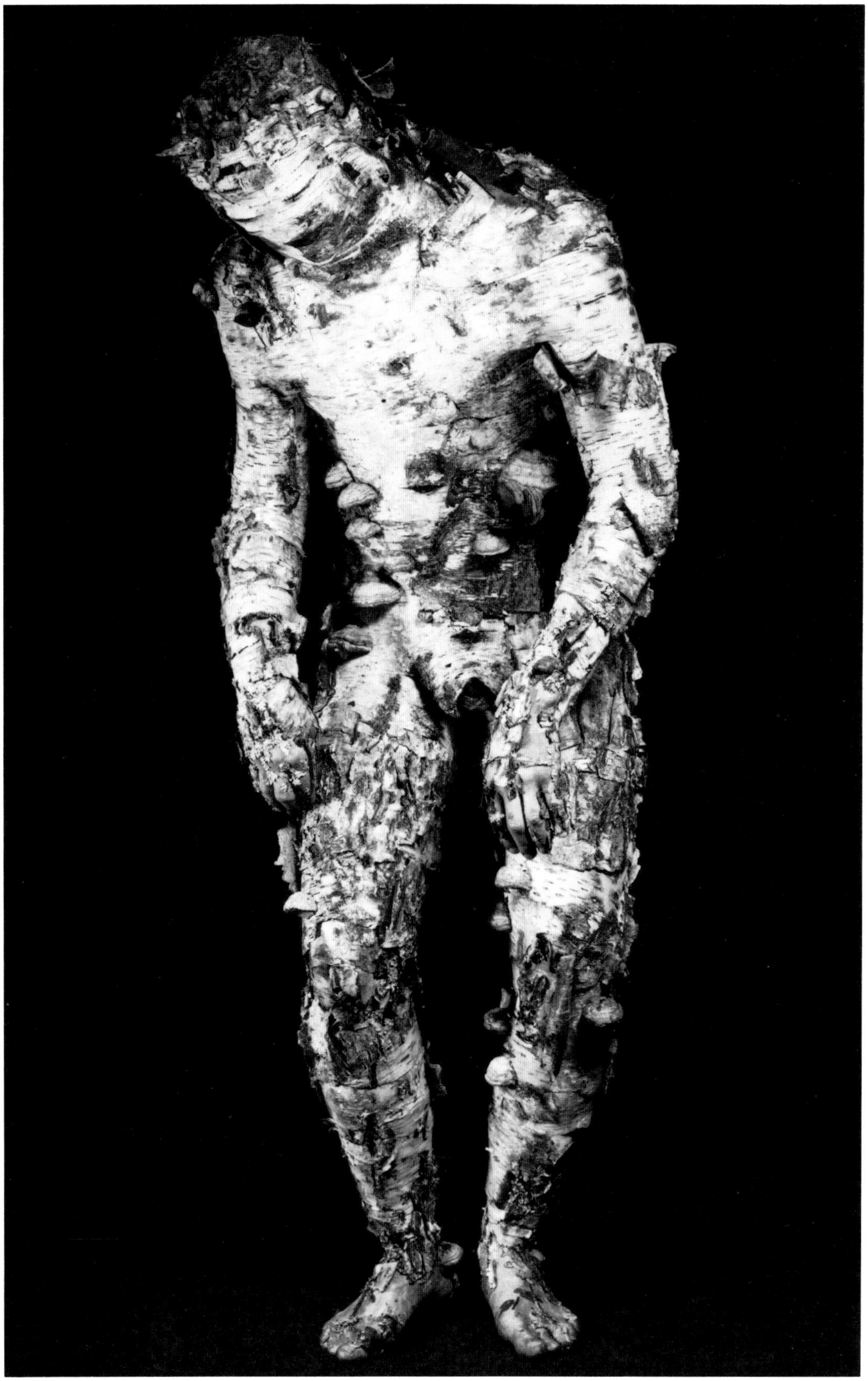

7. Tom Czarnopys, *Somnambulist*, 1985 (cat. no. 7)

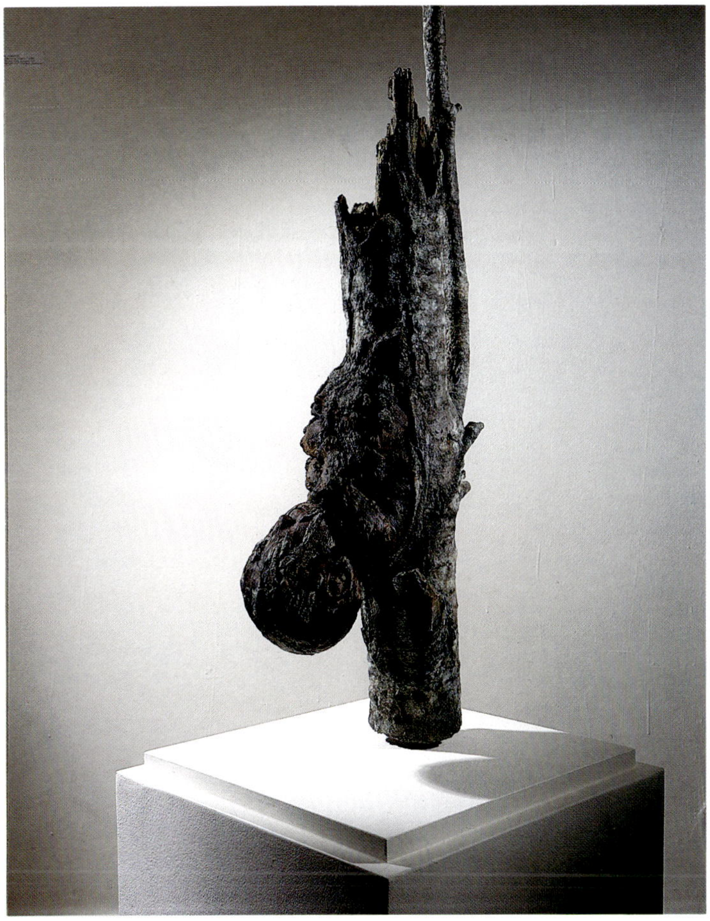

8. Tom Czarnopys, *Birthing Figure* (detail), 1987 (cat. no. 8)

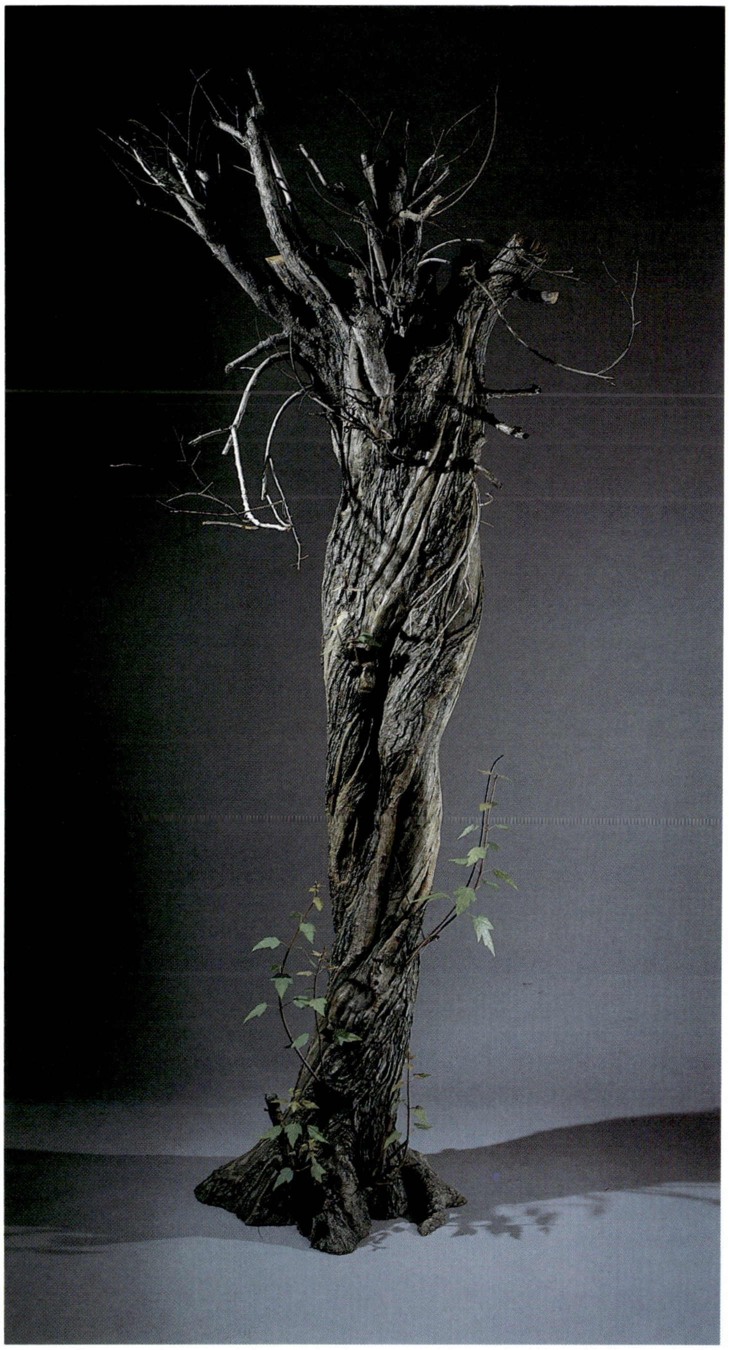

9. Tom Czarnopys, *Pietà*, 1988 (cat. no. 9)

David Deutsch

The landscapes that interest David Deutsch are not the sublime forests of another era, but the fields and meadows that have been tamed by human intervention. There is a highly generalized quality to these images; they are not portraits of specific locales or types of flora, but abstracted ideas about the appearance of cultivated land. Nevertheless, these are sympathetic paintings, representing tough little patches of earth on which organic life continues to survive.

The curved aluminum supports on which the paintings are presented function as frames and evoke a barrage of technological images: the metal frame around the window in a car door, the shape of a television screen, and the border of gray type around a magazine photograph are just a few of the devices through which we encounter the landscape on a daily basis. These are the physical mediators of actual experience.

The gently curved concave surfaces of these paintings draw the viewer into themselves, an effect that is enhanced by the carefully detailed images that compel close attention. This controlled experience refers, perhaps, to an earlier technology—the nineteenth-century panorama, which made use of circular viewing platforms, perfectly consistent perspective, and real as well as immaculately rendered objects. Each panorama was a complete, self-contained, unified structure presenting a coherent worldview in which every fact, object, and idea had its rationale and place. Deutsch, in effect, has preserved small slices of these well-ordered systems, though none of them fits together to form a totality. The grand organization has been lost, and only a few fragments of its meaning are preserved in this work.

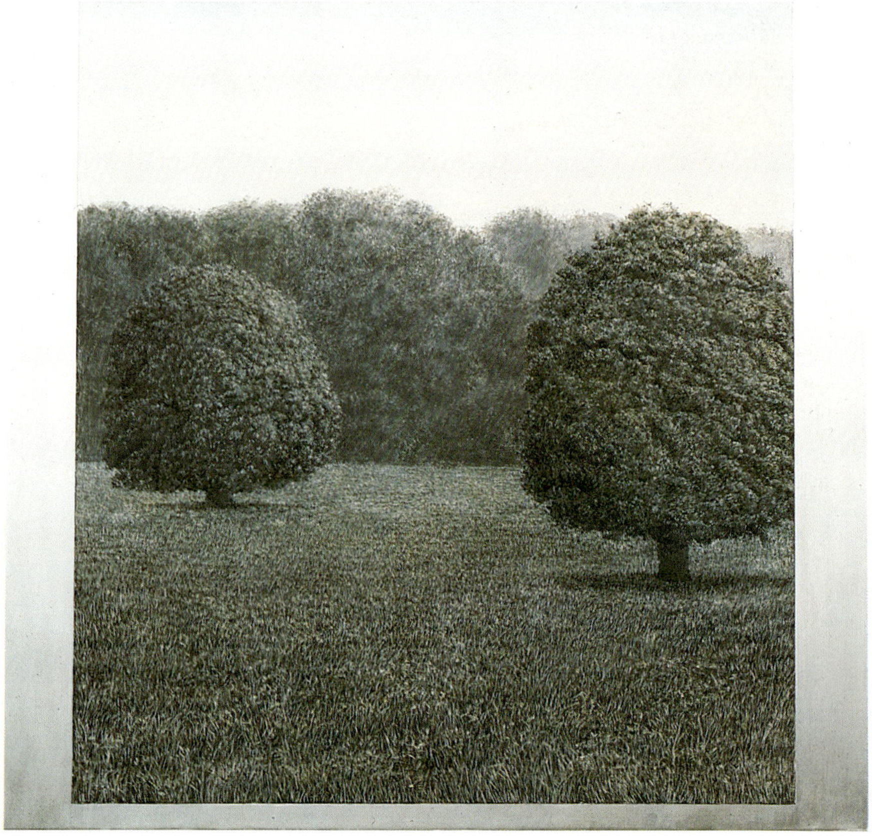

10. David Deutsch, *Trees on Field*, 1986 (cat. no. 10)

Born: 1943, Los Angeles

Education

1968 California Institute of the Arts, Valencia

1966 B.A., University of California, Los Angeles

Selected One-Person Exhibitions

1987 Blum Helman Gallery, New York, "David Deutsch: Recent Work"
Massimo Audiello, New York, "David Deutsch: Works"

1985 Blum Helman Gallery, New York, "David Deutsch"
Blum Helman Gallery, New York, "David Deutsch: New Paintings"

1984 Gallery 5, Stockholm

1982 Annina Nosei Gallery, New York, "David Deutsch"

1981 Annina Nosei Gallery, New York, "David Deutsch"

1980 112 Workshop, Inc., New York
Gagosian/Nosei-Weber Gallery, New York

1972 Michael Walls Gallery, Los Angeles

Selected Group Exhibitions

1987 Art Gallery of Ontario, Toronto, "Selections from the Roger and Myra Davidson Collection"
The Squibb Gallery, Princeton, New Jersey, "Landscape: Real and Imagined"

1986 Orlando Museum of Art at Lock Haven, Florida
The Aldrich Museum of Contemporary Art, Ridgefield, Connecticut, "A Contemporary View of Nature"
Lorence-Monk Gallery, New York, "The Manor in the Landscape" (traveled to Vanguard Gallery, Philadelphia)
The Patrick and Beatrice Haggerty Museum of Art, Marquette University, Milwaukee, "Romanticism and Cynicism in Contemporary Art"
56 Bleeker Gallery Ltd., New York, "Mainly on the Plane"
Herbert H. Lehman College Art Gallery, CUNY New York, "Landscape in the Age of Anxiety"
Luhring, Augustine & Hodes Gallery, New York, "Landscape: Barth, Bleckner, Cucchi, Deutsch, Kiefer, Long, Marden, Smithson"
Michael Kohn Gallery, Los Angeles, "Still Life/Life Still"
San Francisco Museum of Modern Art, "New Visions in Contemporary Art: The RSM Company Collection" (traveled to The Pennsylvania Academy of the Fine Arts, Philadelphia)

1985 Larry Gagosian Gallery, Los Angeles, "Actual Size: An Exhibition of Small Paintings and Sculptures"
Gallery Schlesinger-Boisante, Inc., New York, "Factura"
Luhring, Augustine & Hodes Gallery, New York, "Selected Paintings from Prominent New York Collections"
Hallwalls, Buffalo, "Past and Future Perfect"

1984 Museo Rufino Tamayo, Mexico City, "El Arte Narrativo" (traveled to The Institute for Art and Urban Resources, P.S. 1, Long Island City, New York)
New Math Gallery, New York, "Rediscovered Romanticism in New York City"
Janus Gallery, Los Angeles, "Personal Views"
Holly Solomon Gallery, New York, "The Innovative Landscape: Artists with a New Approach to an Old Tradition"
The Hudson River Museum, Yonkers, New York, "New Vistas: Contemporary American Landscapes"
The Museum of Modern Art, New York, "An International Survey of Recent Painting and Sculpture"
Polytechnic Art Gallery, Newcastle-Upon-Tyne, England, "Newcastle Salutes New York"

1983 Portland Center for the Visual Arts, Oregon, "New Works: The Caduro Collection"
Fuller Goldeen Gallery, San Francisco, "Perspectives of Landscape"
Museum of Art, Carnegie Institute, Pittsburgh, "New York Painting Today"
John Weber Gallery, New York, "Science Fiction"
Clocktower, The Institute for Art and Urban Resources, New York, "Habitats"

1982 Municipal Gallery, Modena, Italy, "Transavantgardia, Italia/America"
Hayden Gallery, Massachusetts Institute of Technology, Cambridge, "Great Big Drawings"

1981 Procter Art Center, Bard College, New York, "Figures Drawings"
Edward Thorp Gallery, New York, "Landscapes"

1972 Kassel, West Germany, "Documenta 6"

1970 La Jolla Museum of Contemporary Art, California, "Directions: Anti-Materialism"

1969 Montgomery Gallery, Pomona College, Claremont, California, "Six Attitudes"

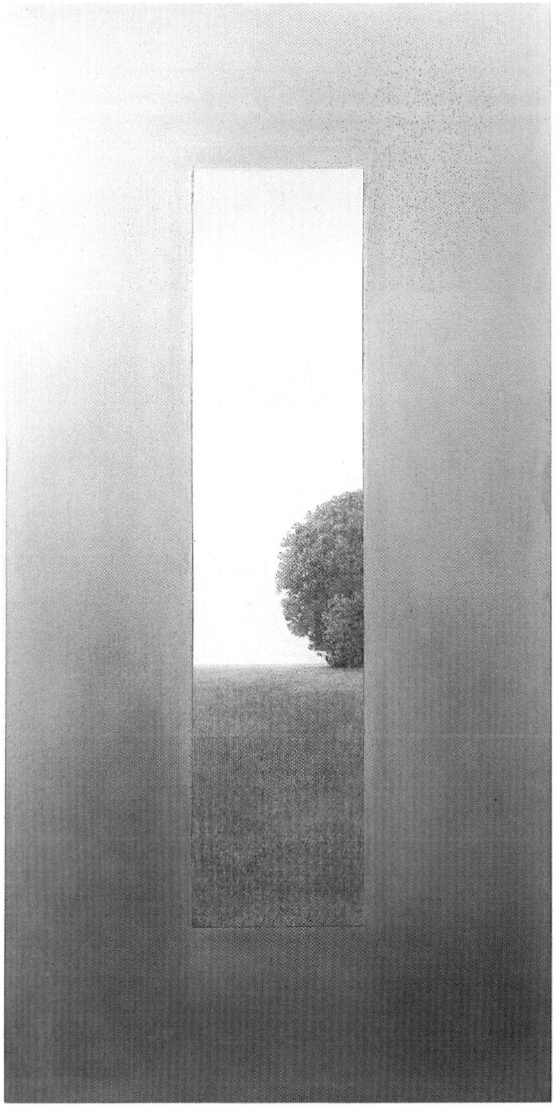

11. David Deutsch, *Strike Section*, 1986-88 (cat. no. 11)

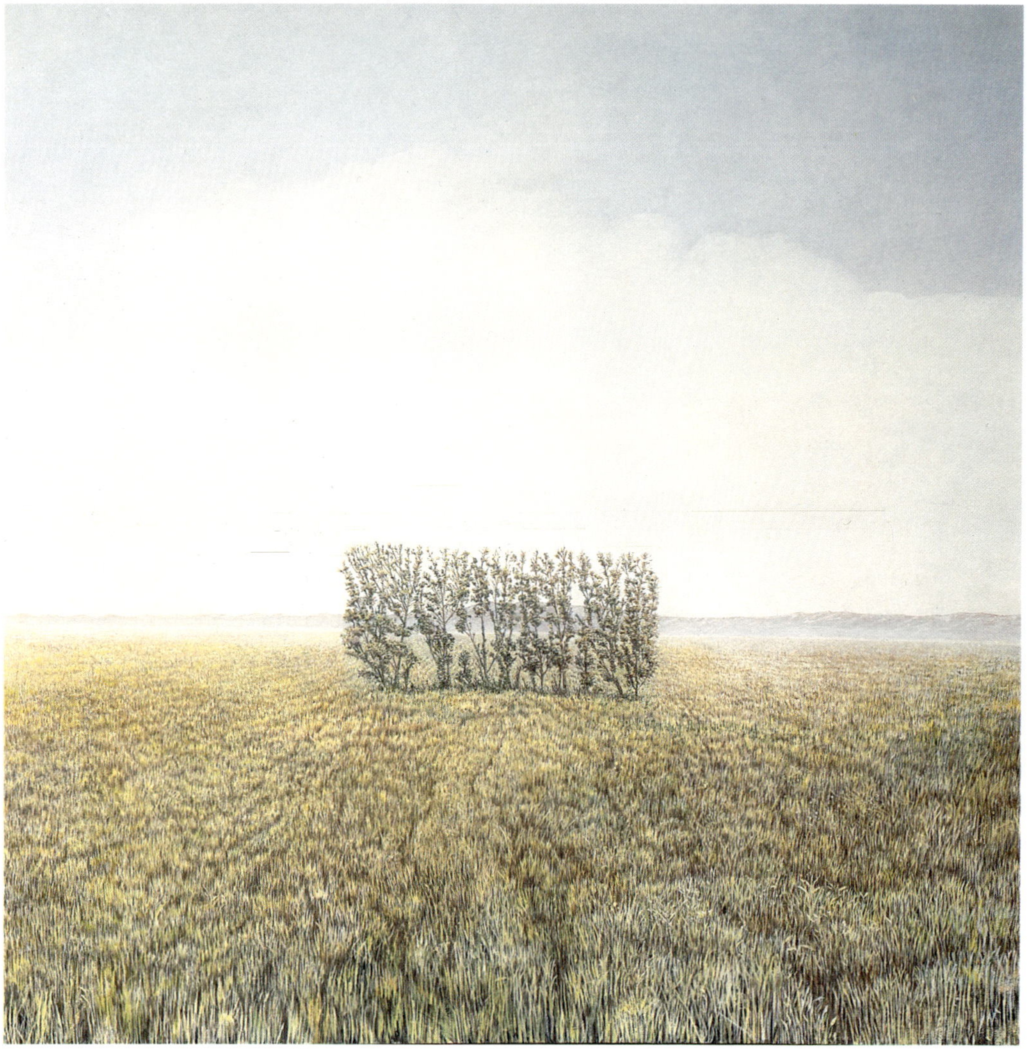

12. David Deutsch, *Animation Regionale*, 1987 (cat. no. 12)

Jeanne Dunning

At first glance Jeanne Dunning's photographs appear to be straightforward, almost scientific, studies of exquisite details from the natural landscape. On closer inspection it quickly becomes apparent, however, that the rich blue sky is actually a studio backdrop and that the artist has very carefully arranged the objects and the light in her compositions. This recognition is very similar to the semiconscious process by which readers identify doctored or "enhanced" photographs in newspapers and magazines; the artifice is acknowledged and, if its intent does not appear to be dishonest, it is disregarded. As Dunning recently told a friend, "my intention was not to fool people into thinking that these photographs were taken outdoors, but to fool them only long enough for them to realize that they are often fooled."

The inscriptions on the surfaces of these works appear to identify the subject, but here again initial perceptions are misleading. The Latin and English names of an insect that typically camouflages itself in the depicted environment are inscribed across the surface of each image; this, of course, implies that the insect is also included in the photograph. When, on careful scrutiny, it becomes apparent that no animate life forms are present, the viewer is left to wonder about the reliability of language and the value of scientific classification, as well as the authenticity of photography.

The frames that Dunning has carefully selected to accompany her photographs add yet another layer of representation and meaning to her work. The ornamental patterns of each frame echo the forms and textures of the bark, twigs, or leaves in the photograph, thereby re-representing the subject at an additional remove. Because the frames evoke a Victorian aesthetic, they also carry connotations of the conventions and value systems of the late nineteenth century, and a conscious awareness of the history, sociology, psychology, and epistemology that shape perception.

Born: 1960, Granby, Connecticut

Education
1985 M.F.A., The School of the Art Institute of Chicago
1982 B.A., Oberlin College, Ohio

Awards
1987 Special Assistance Grant, Illinois Arts Council

Selected One-Person Exhibitions
1987 Feature, Chicago

Selected Group Exhibitions
1987 Feature, Chicago, "Knew"
University of Illinois Galleries, Normal, "Anxious Objects"
Chicago, "The Non-Spiritual in Art—Abstract Painting 1985-????"
Wolff Gallery, New York
First Street Forum, St. Louis, "Beyond the Image"
University of Wisconsin-Milwaukee, "Postmodernism: A Spectacle of Reflexivity"
Feature, Chicago, "Nature"
1986 Randolph Street Gallery, Chicago, "Dull Edge"
Feature, Chicago, "Promises, Promises" (traveled to Pyramid Arts Center, Rochester, New York; CAGE, Cincinnati, Ohio)
Artemisia Gallery, Chicago, "Women Sculptors"
1985 MoMing Gallery, Chicago, "Second Annual Juried Drawing Show" Randolph Street Gallery, Chicago, "Randolph Street Gallery Outdoor Installations"
1840 West Hubbard, Chicago, "1840 Show"
1982 Allen Memorial Art Museum, Oberlin College, Ohio, "Oberlin Artists"

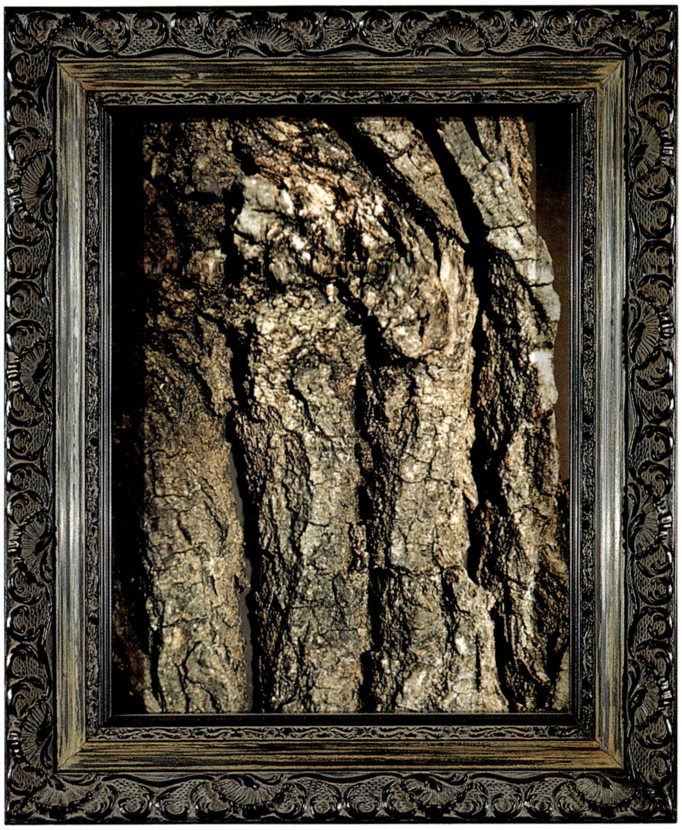

13. Jeanne Dunning, *Untitled (bark)*, 1987 (cat. no. 13)

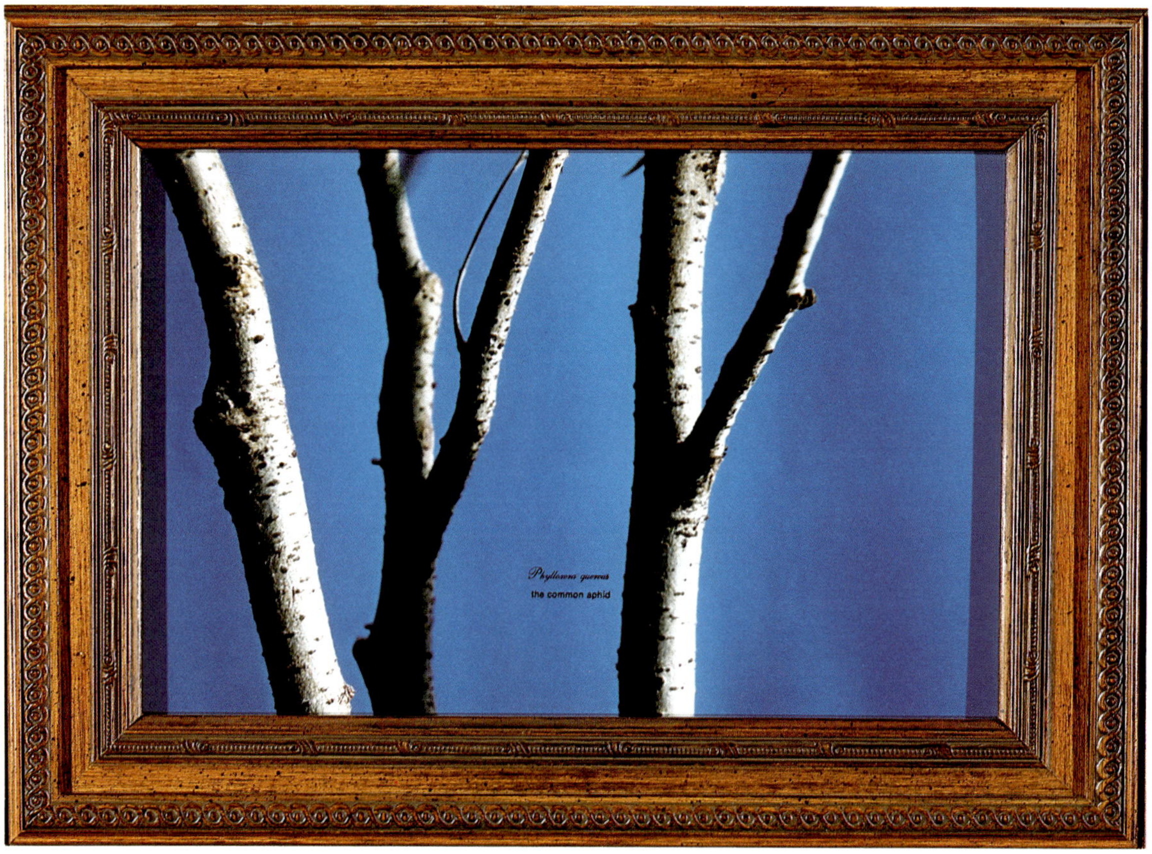

14. Jeanne Dunning, *Untitled (branches)*, 1987 (cat. no. 14)

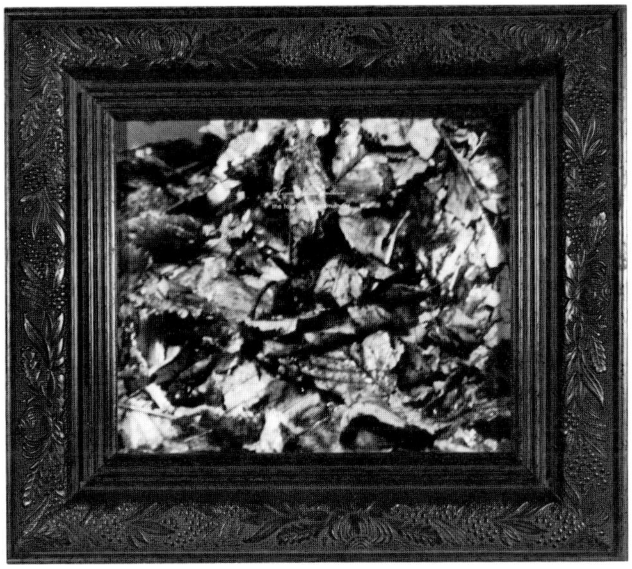

15. Jeanne Dunning, *Untitled (dead leaves)*, 1987 (cat. no. 15)

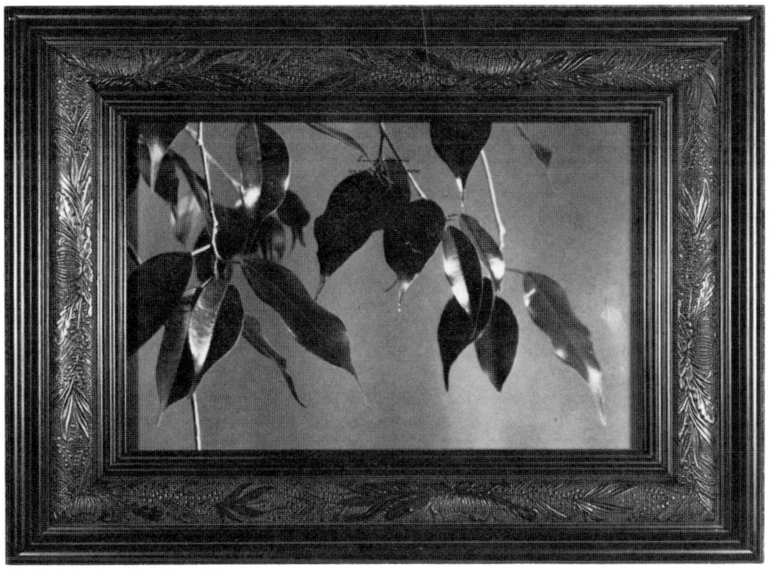

16. Jeanne Dunning, *Untitled (leaves)*, 1987 (cat. no. 16)

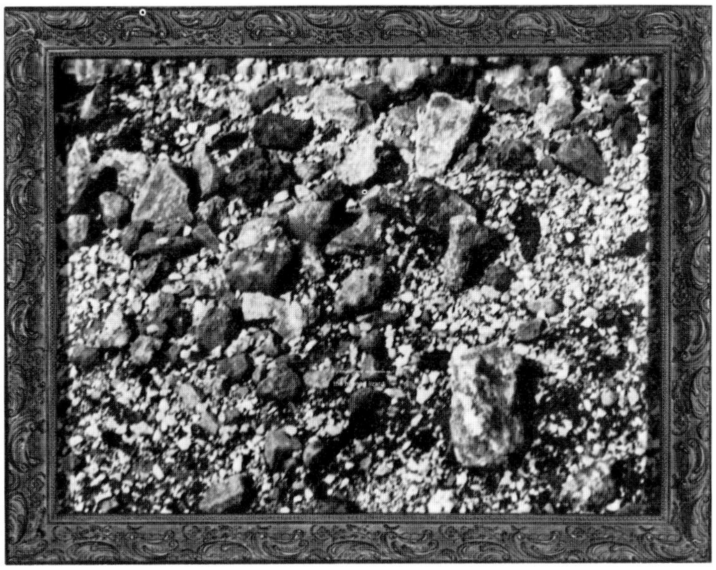

17. Jeanne Dunning, *Untitled (rocks)*, 1987 (cat. no. 17)

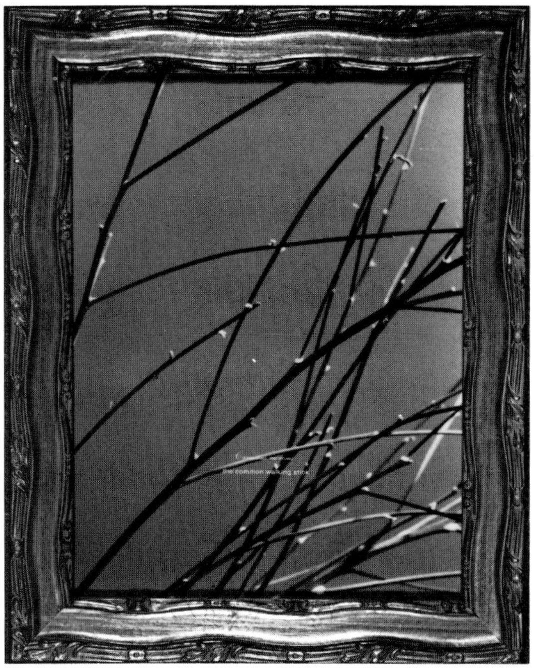

18. Jeanne Dunning, *Untitled (stems)*, 1987 (cat. no. 18)

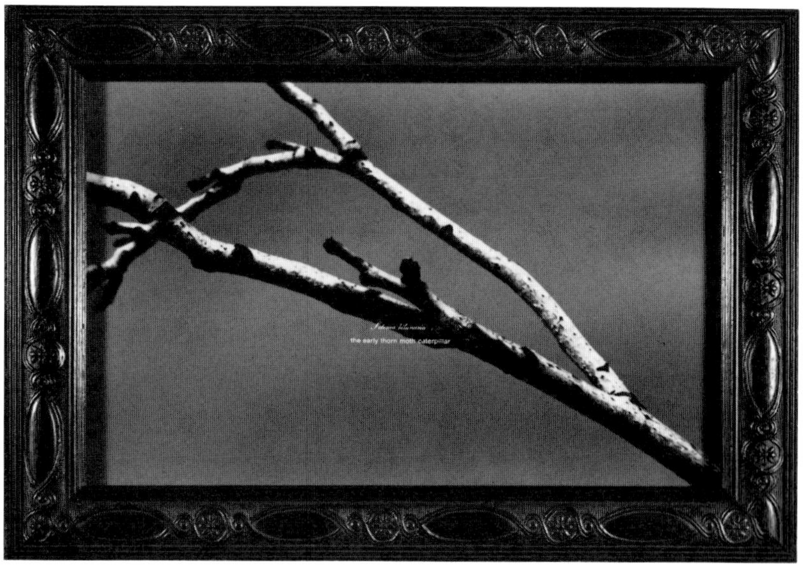

19. Jeanne Dunning, *Untitled (stick)*, 1987 (cat no. 19)

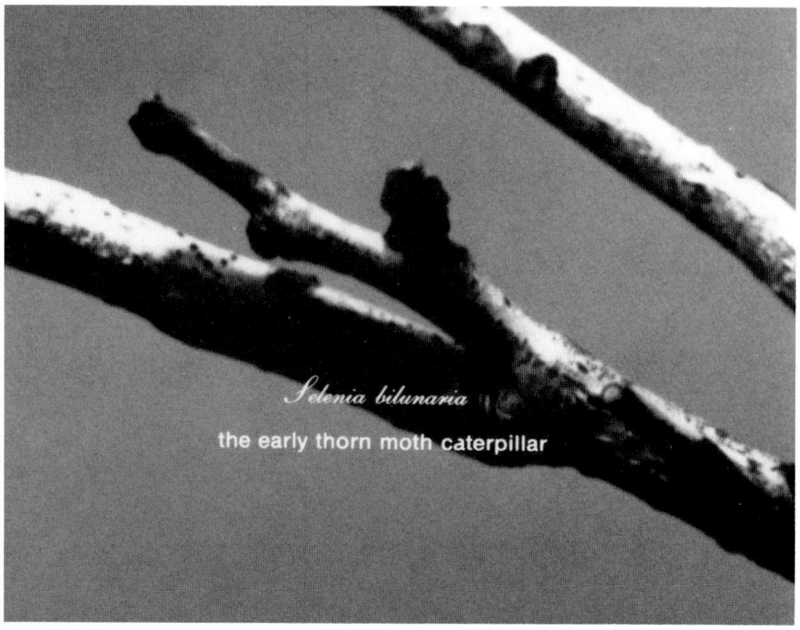

20. Jeanne Dunning, *Untitled (stick)* (detail), 1987 (cat. no. 19)

Peter Fleps

The windswept skies, regal mountains, and spectral trees of Peter Fleps's landscapes are presented on sculpted pedestals or on sheets of gleaming metal that evoke a religious context. In shape and format these framing devices resemble lecterns and altarpieces, connoting divine experience as well as moral lessons. It is also interesting to note that an altar is a place of sacrifice, however ritualized; these landscapes seem to be offered in all of these ways—as sources of spiritual elevation, as sermons on the preservation of precious resources, and as oblations for unnatural uses of the land.

As a conceptual metaphor, a pedestal elevates whatever it contains, lifting it out of the ordinary and into the realm of the ideal. Fleps's landscapes do conform to popular romantic ideals which perceive florid sunsets and sultry full moons as ultimate expressions of the transcendent power of nature. Both the cultural significance and the banality of these iconic images are accentuated by the artist's sly choice of materials.

The formica pedestal on which *Land* (cat. no. 21) is displayed mimics marble, a highly valued natural material with a long tradition in western civilization. In addition, the *faux* marble patterns imitate the slashing forms and cloudy colors of the stormy sky in the painting. A synthetic material is used here to parody a synthetic image, calling into question the entire value system that esteems nature but does not preserve it. Since scarcity increases the economic worth of any commodity, this can also be seen as a wry commentary on the disjunction between the value of the experience of nature, which decreases as natural sites are exploited, and the value of natural products, which increases as they become rarer.

Born: 1955, Montgomery, Alabama

Education

1977 B.F.A., Nova Scotia College of Art and Design, Halifax
1974-76 Hartford Art School, University of Hartford, Connecticut

Selected One-Person Exhibitions

1986 Jack Shainman Gallery, New York
1985 Jack Shainman Gallery, Washington, D.C., "Two Places"
1980 Trotech/McIntosh Gallery, Washington, D.C.

Selected Group Exhibitions

1986 The Aldrich Museum of Contemporary Art, Ridgefield, Connecticut, "A View of Nature"
Hirshhorn Museum and Sculpture Garden, Washington, D.C., "Directions 1986"
Jack Shainman Gallery, Washington, D.C., "Invitational Exhibition"
1984 616 E Street, Washington, D.C., ACE Group Exhibition
1981 Hallwalls, Buffalo, "Fictive Victims"
1978 The Corcoran Gallery of Art, Washington, D.C., "21st Area Exhibition: Sculpture"

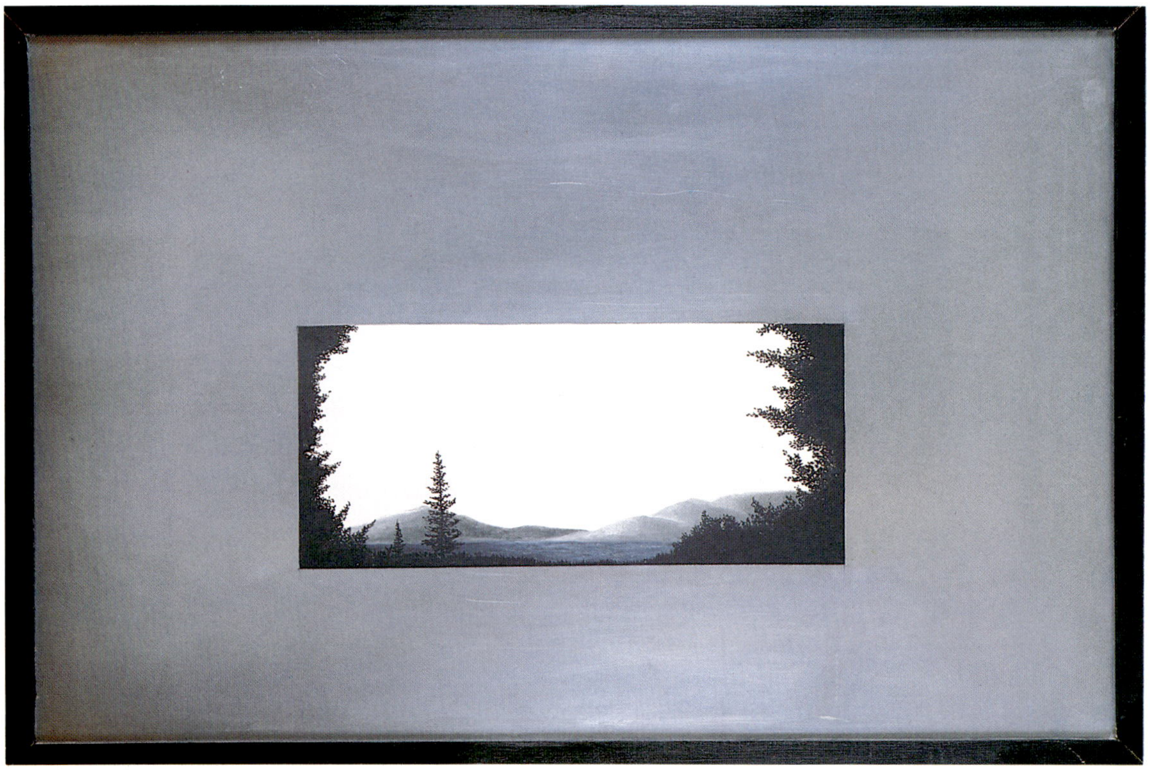

21. Peter Fleps, *Untitled*, 1985 (cat. no. 20)

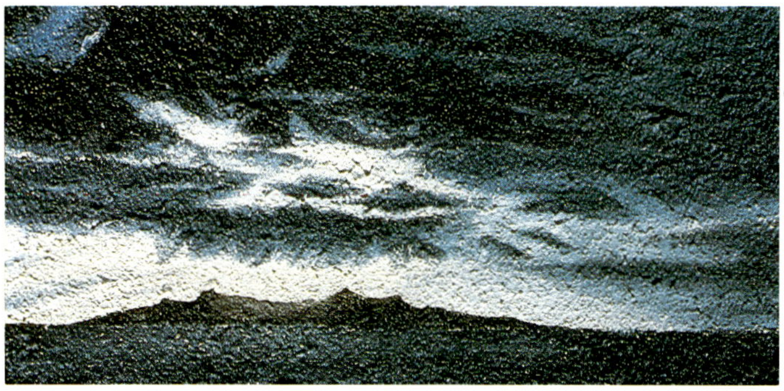

23. Peter Fleps, *Land* (detail), 1986 (cat. no. 21)

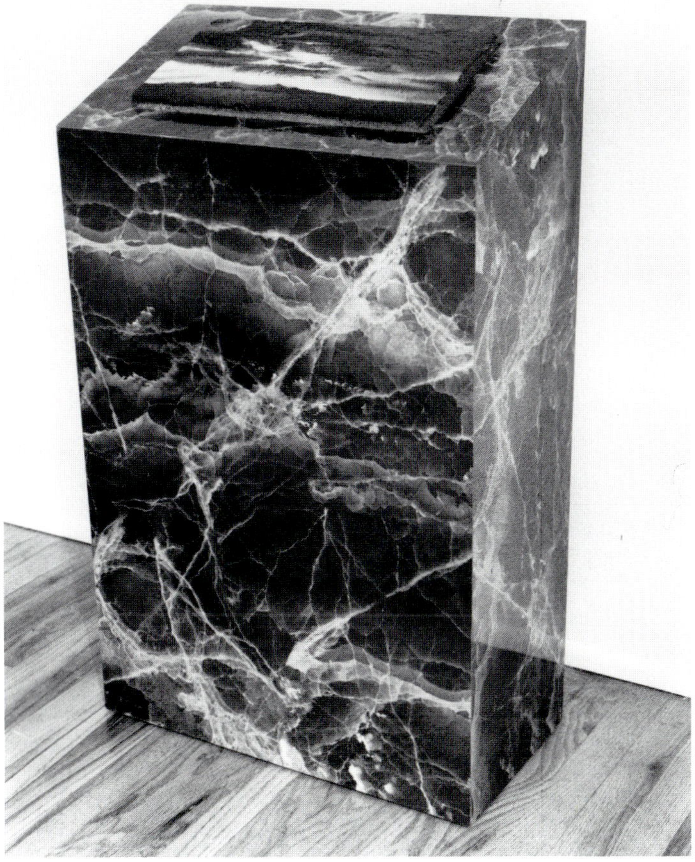

22. Peter Fleps, *Land*, 1986 (cat. no. 21)

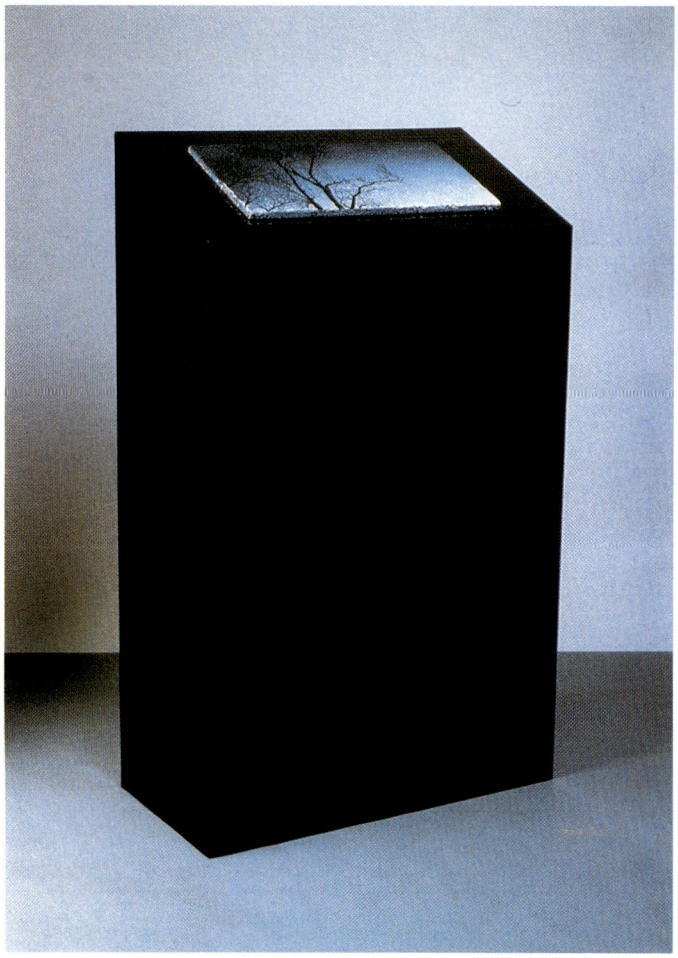

24. Peter Fleps, *Law*, 1986 (cat. no. 22)

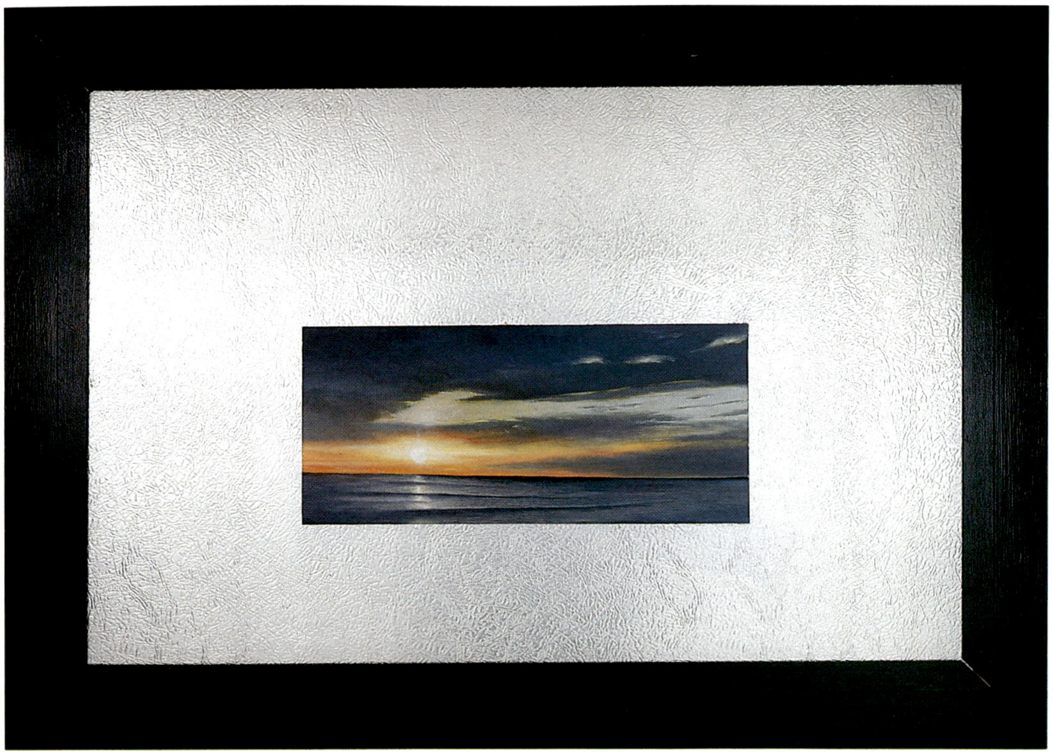

25. Peter Fleps, *One Morning*, 1986 (cat. no. 23)

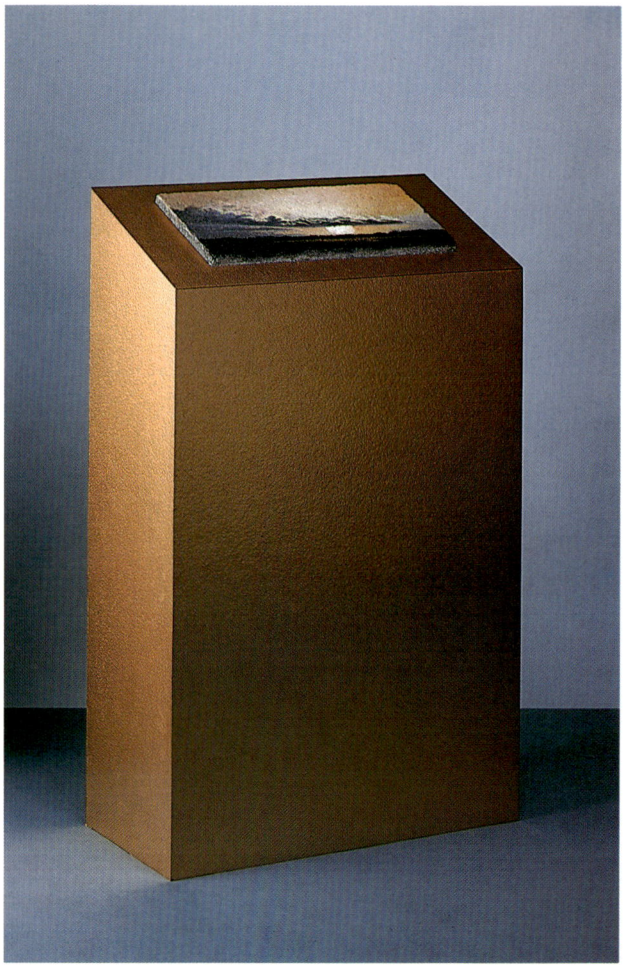

26. Peter Fleps, *Subordinate*, 1986 (cat. no. 24)

April Gornik

The absence of human activity is particularly notable in April Gornik's theatrical landscapes which are staged and lit for dramatic action. Although the effects of weather and light form the basis for an engaging narrative, histrionic rocks and cloud formations play the leading roles. Gornik does not set the scene for comedy or light romance, but for morality tales with deep psychological undertones. Threatening skies, menacing storms, and advancing dusk bode meanings that exceed the import of meteorological phenomena.

Gornik works from memory and dreams, as well as from photographs and sketches of natural sites, and her schematic compositions reflect this artifice. The nearly symmetrical pairing of ragged cloud formations in *Triple Smoke* (cat. no. 26), one of the artist's favorite compositional devices, reflects a willful determination that implicates the audience in its control of the natural imagery. This device also serves to block the view, which for all of its vastness remains claustrophobic.

Sublime nature, seen through Gornik's cinematic vision, is an inscrutable, disinterested force that enacts its own intense drama, neither inviting nor prohibiting human observation or participation. Oblivious to its audience, it nevertheless reveals its grandeur, and reinfuses our jaded perception of the natural world with power and strangeness.

Born: 1953, Cleveland

Education

1976 B.F.A., Nova Scotia College of Art and Design, Halifax
1971-75 Cleveland Institute of Art

Selected One-Person Exhibitions

1988 The Sable-Castelli Gallery, Toronto
1985 Galerie Springer, West Berlin, "April Gornik: Bilder und Pastelle"
Institute of Contemporary Art, Boston
1984 Texas Gallery, Houston
The New Gallery of Contemporary Art, Cleveland
1983 Edward Thorp Gallery, New York
1982 University of Colorado Art Galleries, Boulder

Selected Group Exhibitions

1987 Art Gallery, Long Island University, Southampton, New York, "The Masters II"
The Rockwell Museum, Corning, New York, "Boundless Realism: Contemporary Landscape Painting of the West"
Barbara Mathes Gallery, New York, "Disquiet in the Landscape"
Whitney Museum of American Art, Stamford, Connecticut, "The New Romantic Landscape"
Squibb Gallery, Princeton, New Jersey, "Landscapes: Real & Imagined"
The Aldrich Museum of Contemporary Art, Ridgefield, Connecticut, "A View of Nature"
1986 Herbert H. Lehman College Art Gallery, CUNY New York, "Landscape in the Age of Anxiety"
Michael Kohn Gallery, Los Angeles, "Still Life/Life Still"
Phoenix Art Museum, "New Narrative Painting: Selections from the Metropolitan Museum of Art"
Contemporary Arts Center, New Orleans, "Landscape, Seascape, Cityscape, 1960-1985"
The Brooklyn Museum, New York, "Public and Private: American Prints Today"
The Corcoran Gallery of Art, Washington, D.C., "Spectrum, Natural Settings"
1985 The Taft Museum, Cincinnati, Ohio, "Night Lights"
Koplin Gallery, Los Angeles, "Views"
Lorence-Monk Gallery, New York, "Real Surreal"
Sordoni Art Gallery, Wilkes College, Wilkes-Barre, Pennsylvania, "The New Expressive Landscape"
The Henry Art Gallery, Seattle, "Luminist Show"
Tweed Gallery, Plainfield, New Jersey, "The Elements: Weather in Art"
Dart Gallery, Chicago, "Night Lights"
Janus Gallery, Los Angeles, "Personal Visions"
1984 Bienale de Venezia, Venice, "Paradise Lost/Paradise Regained: American Visions of the New Decade in the 40th International Art Exposition" (traveled to Lisbon, Madrid, Athens, Belgrade, and Budapest)
Sidney Janis Gallery, New York, "A Celebration of American Women Artists: Part II: The Recent Generation"
The Hudson River Museum, Yonkers, New York, "New Vistas: Contemporary American Landscapes"
1983 Ben Shahn Galleries, The William Patterson College of New Jersey, Wayne
Kathryn Markel Gallery, New York, "Contemporary Light"

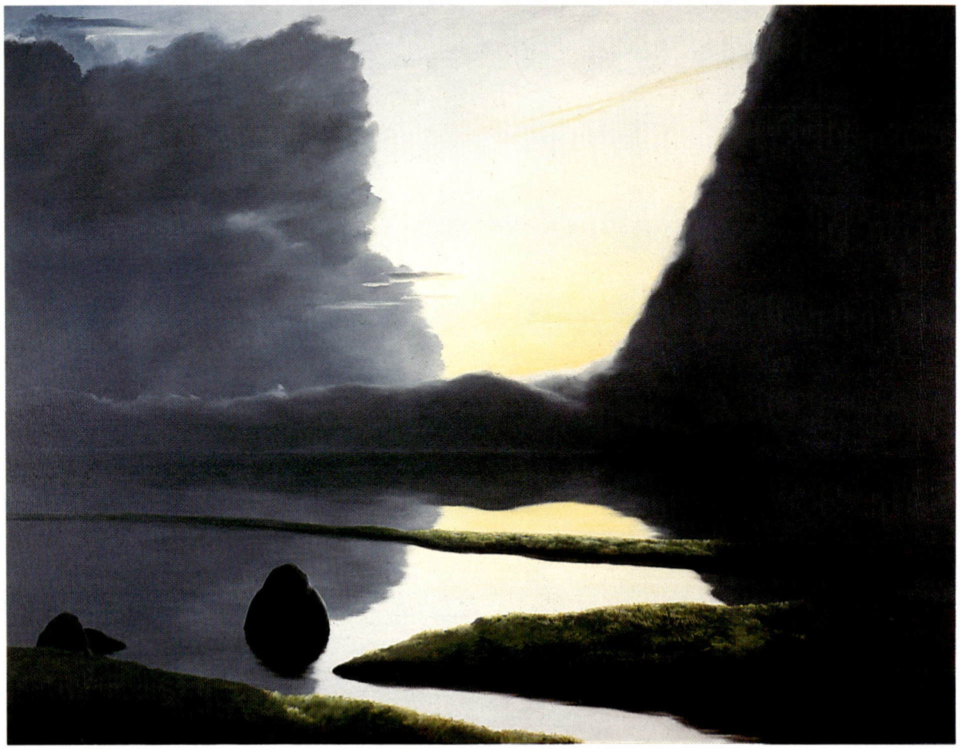

27. April Gornik, *Corridor*, 1984 (cat. no. 25)

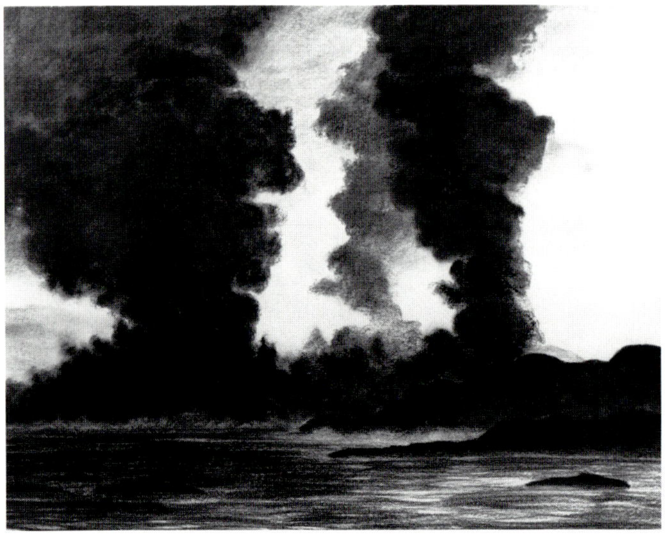

28. April Gornik, *Triple Smoke*, 1986 (cat. no. 26)

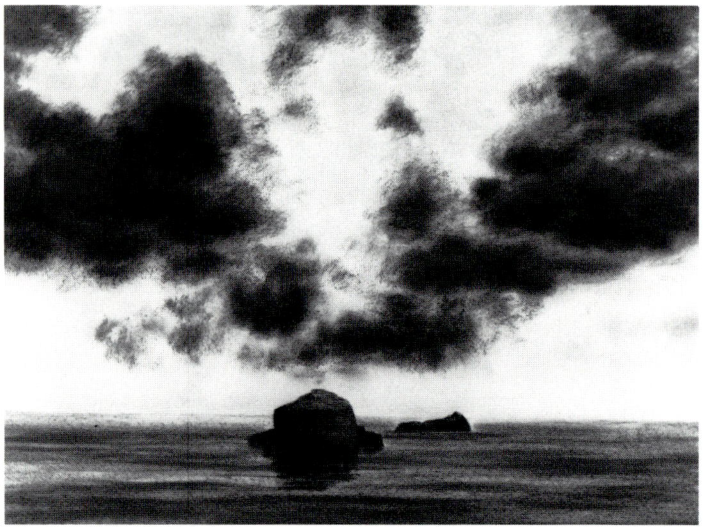

29. April Gornik, *Biarritz*, 1987 (cat. no. 27)

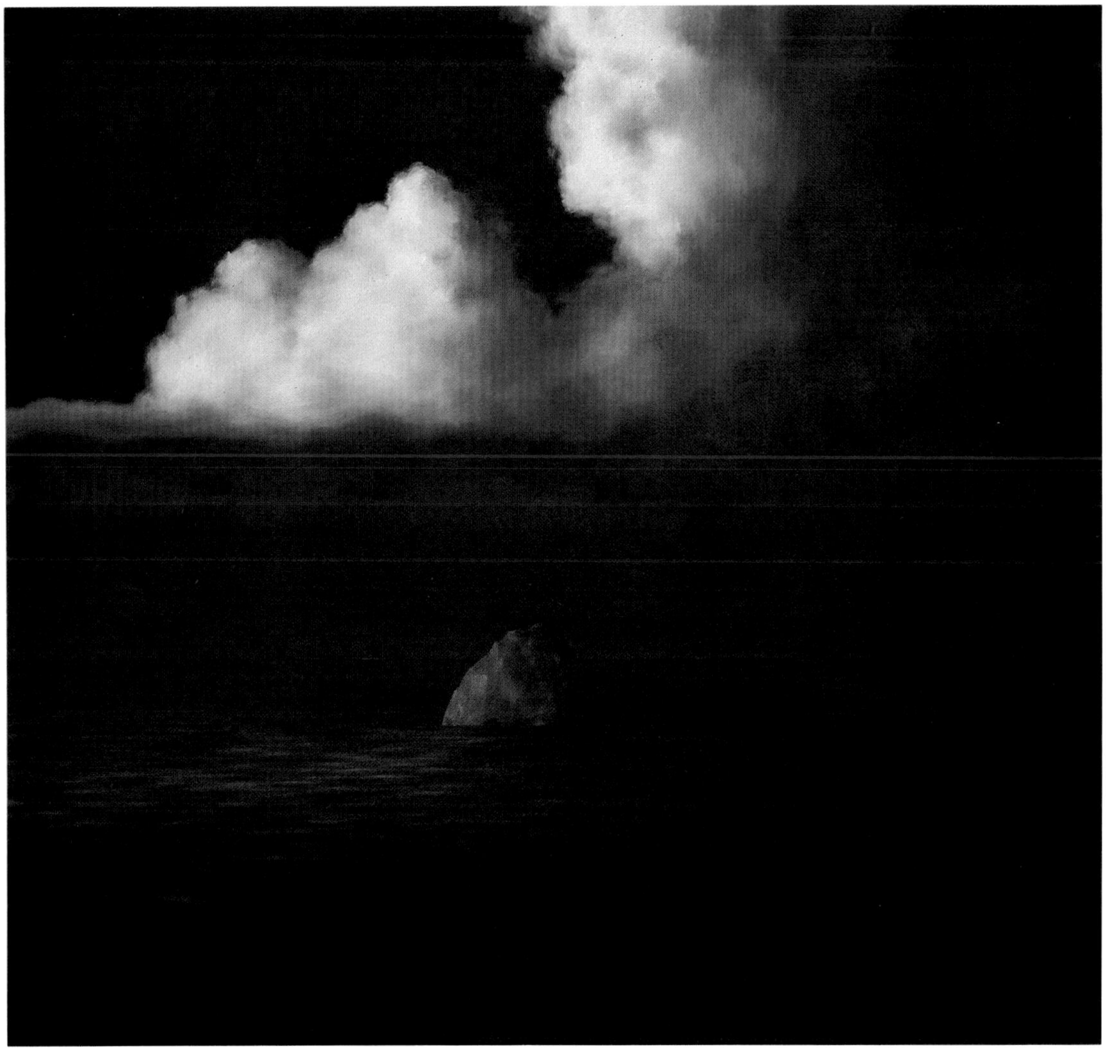

30. April Gornik, *The Sea at Night*, 1987 (cat. no. 28)

Robert Helm

Although Robert Helm depicts contrived situations within natural settings, rather than untouched landscapes, his work is strongly evocative of the natural history of this planet. The enigmatic combinations of images in these paintings suggest the juxtapositions that occur on a beach after a high tide; objects with no logical connection to each other appear inevitably and inextricably grouped together by the accidental processes of nature. The birds that inhabit Helm's pictorial spaces are the metaphysical descendants of LopLop, Max Ernst's preconscious alterego. Their existence seems as simple and devoid of desire as that of the wind that ruffles the water or the planks that alternate with the natural terrain.

This sense of the equivalence of all natural things is enhanced by the materials Helm uses, which often are literally recycled. Whether he finds his boards in old buildings, antique furniture, or lumberyards, they maintain their own history and identity as they are transformed into something new. These wooden surfaces are sometimes painted and sometimes composed of intricate marquetry, but they always create credible illusions of space and depth. It is the light in these works that blurs the distinction between various modes of representation. Casting *trompe l'oeil* shadows of paint and inlaid wood, it models and highlights the forms, bathing them in a hyper-real glow. The architectural frames are made of the same warmly colored wood, but are inlaid with abstract geometric patterns, references to conscious, rational activity. The natural sepia tones of the wood evoke old photographs and other faded images of loss; the artist's skill, and the durability of his craftsmanship, however, seem to refute the certain decay of his materials as well as the subjects and states of mind that they portray. In their stillness, strangeness, and permanence, these paintings appear to belong to the natural world.

Born: 1943, Wallace, Idaho

Education

1969 M.F.A., Washington State University, Pullman

1967 B.A., Washington State University, Pullman

Awards

1978 Deutscher Akademischer Austausch dienst (D.A.A.D.), West Berlin

Selected One-Person Exhibitions

1987 Edward Thorp Gallery, New York, "Robert Helm"

1984 Contemporary Arts Museum, Houston, "Robert Helm: Recent Work"

1983 Seattle Art Museum, "Documents Northwest: Robert Helm"

1982 Galerie Redmann, West Berlin

1978 Nicholas Wilder Gallery, Los Angeles

1977 Faith and Charity in Hope Gallery, Idaho

1976 Nicholas Wilder Gallery, Los Angeles

1974 Museum of Art, Washington State University, Pullman

1970 Nebraska Wesleyan University, Lincoln

Selected Group Exhibitions

1988 Neuberger Museum, State University of New York, Purchase, "Focus on the Collection"

1987 Whitney Museum of American Art, New York, "Biennale 1987"

1982 Düsseldorf, "Art Fair, 82"
Cologne, "Art Fair, 82"
Basel, "Art Fair, 82"

1980 Middendorf-Lane Gallery, Washington, D.C. "Tableaux, an American Selection"

1977 Paris, "Biennale 10"

1975 Missoula Museum of the Arts, Montana, "Concepts and Executions of 8 Sculptors"
Galerie Giancarla Bocchi, Milan
Museum of Art, Washington State University, Pullman, "Northwest Sculpture"

1974 Peter Whyte Gallery, Banff, Canada

1973 Washington State Governor's Invitational Show, Olympia

1972 Ashland College, Ohio, "Contemporary Painting and Sculpture Invitational"

1971 Brena Gallery, Denver

1969 Cherry Cowles Memorial Museum, Spokane, Washington, "Northwest Annual"

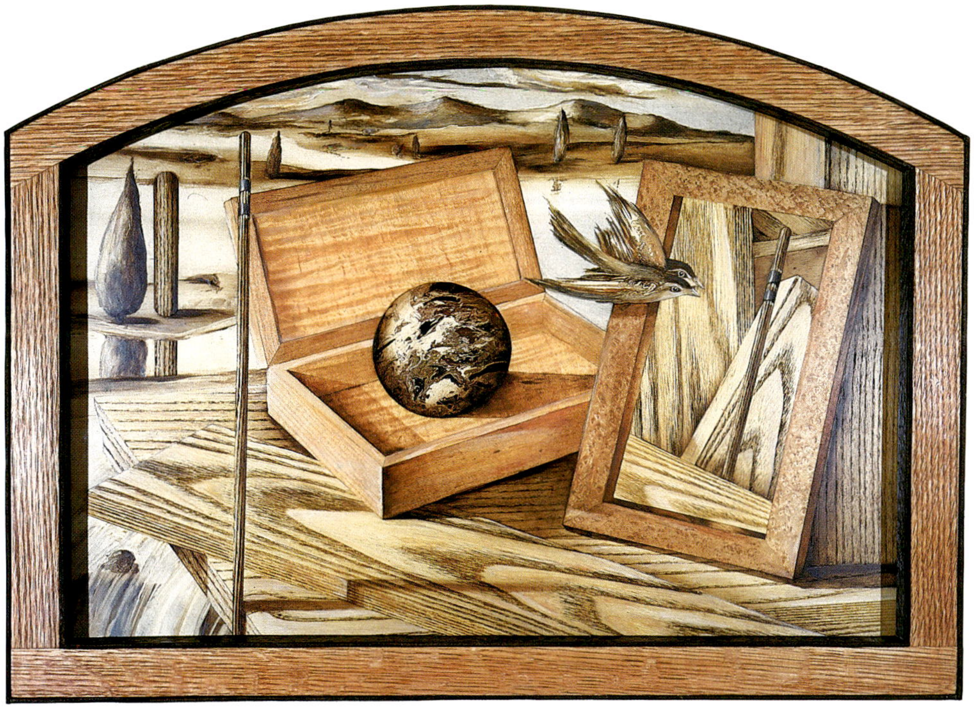

31. Robert Helm, *Spring Thaw*, 1985 (cat. no. 29)

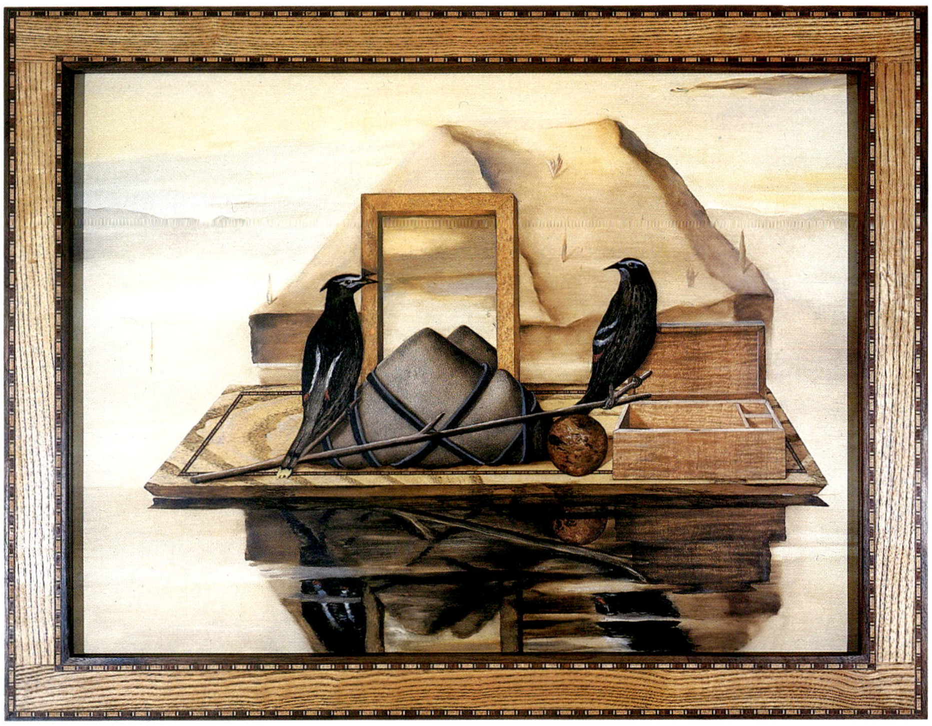

32. Robert Helm, *Falling Hour*, 1986 (cat. no. 30)

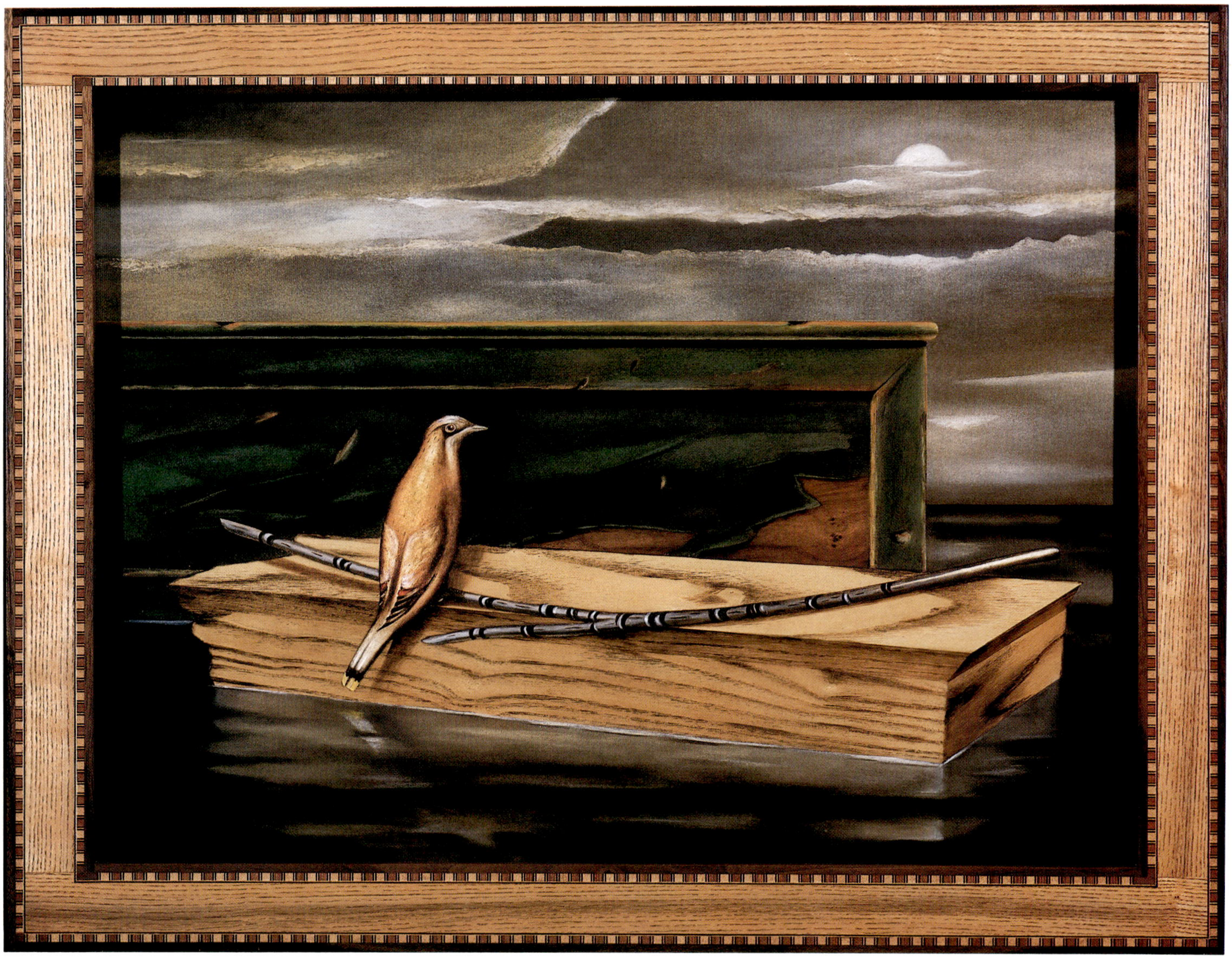

33. Robert Helm, *Rain Shadow*, 1987 (cat. no. 31)

Mark Innerst

The subjects of Mark Innerst's paintings are not scenes that appear in the natural world, but views copied from nineteenth-century paintings, dioramas in natural history museums, and even lampshades—sources that have been impoverished by too frequent reproduction and repetition. The deliberate banality of these appropriated images calls attention to the way the landscape has become an empty symbol for natural grandeur which no longer exists. By painting them with skill and care, Innerst has infused his subjects with new meaning, however small: the simple desire to recover their lost significance.

The extremely small size of these paintings further diminishes the sublime heroism of the views on which they are based. These landscapes do not overwhelm, but are confined and controlled by conventions of representation and by overscale frames that exaggerate the preciousness of the imagery.

The nostalgia inherent in these paintings is underscored by the neo-Victorian frames that Innerst constructs for his paintings, and his stylistic references are as sentimental as his frames: Impressionist color and brushwork or layers of brown varnish describe a world that is irrevocably past. Innerst's use of nostalgia skirts the boundaries of kitsch—that stylishly retro arena in which emotions are manipulated by well-worn signs without ever being genuinely experienced. It is the artist's virtuoso command of the craft and materials of painting that ultimately keeps this work from crossing that line and gives it an air of authenticity.

Born: 1957, York, Pennsylvania

Education

1980 B.F.A., Kutztown, Pennsylvania

Selected One-Person Exhibitions

1988 University Galleries, Illinois State University, Normal, "Mark Innerst: Landscape and Beyond" (1989 traveled to University Art Galleries, Wright State University, Dayton, Ohio; Contemporary Arts Museum, Houston; Museum of Contemporary Art, Chicago; Freedman Gallery, Albright College, Reading, Pennsylvania)
Curt Marcus Gallery, New York

1986 Curt Marcus Gallery, New York

1985 James Mayor Gallery, London
Robert Frazer Gallery, London

1984 Grace Borgenicht Gallery, New York

1982 The Kitchen, New York

Selected Group Exhibitions

1987 Visual Arts Museum, New York, "Still Life: Beyond Tradition"

1986 Bienale de Venezia, Venice, "42nd International Art Exposition"
Société des Expositions du Palais des Beaux-Arts, Brussels, "Au Coeur du Maelstrom"
Herbert H. Lehman College Art Gallery, CUNY New York, "Landscape in the Age of Anxiety"

1985 Curt Marcus Gallery, New York, "Inaugural Exhibition"
University Art Museum, University of California at Santa Barbara, "Scapes" (traveled to The Art Gallery, University of Hawaii, Honolulu)
Solomon R. Guggenheim Museum, New York, "New Horizons in American Art"
Museo Rufino Tamayo, Mexico City, "Nueva pintura narrative: coleccion del Metropolitan Museum of Art, Nueva York"
Larry Gagosian Gallery, Los Angeles, "Actual Size"
Lorence-Monk Gallery, New York, "Real Surreal"

1984 Institute of Contemporary Art, Boston, "Currents"
The Museum of Modern Art, New York, "An International Survey of Recent Painting and Sculpture"
Palazzo Ducale, Gubbio, Italy, "New Landscape Painting"
Museo Rufino Tamayo, Mexico City, "New Narrative Paintings"
Larry Gagosian Gallery, Los Angeles, "An Exhibition of New Painting and Sculpture from the Lower East Side"
Nature Morte, New York, "Civilization and Landscape of Discontent"
Indianapolis Museum of Art, Indiana, "Paintings and Sculpture Today 1984"

1983 Grace Borgenicht Gallery, New York, "Invitational Exhibition"

1982 White Columns, New York, "Rellife Magazine"

1981 Hallwalls Gallery, Buffalo, "Fictive Victims"

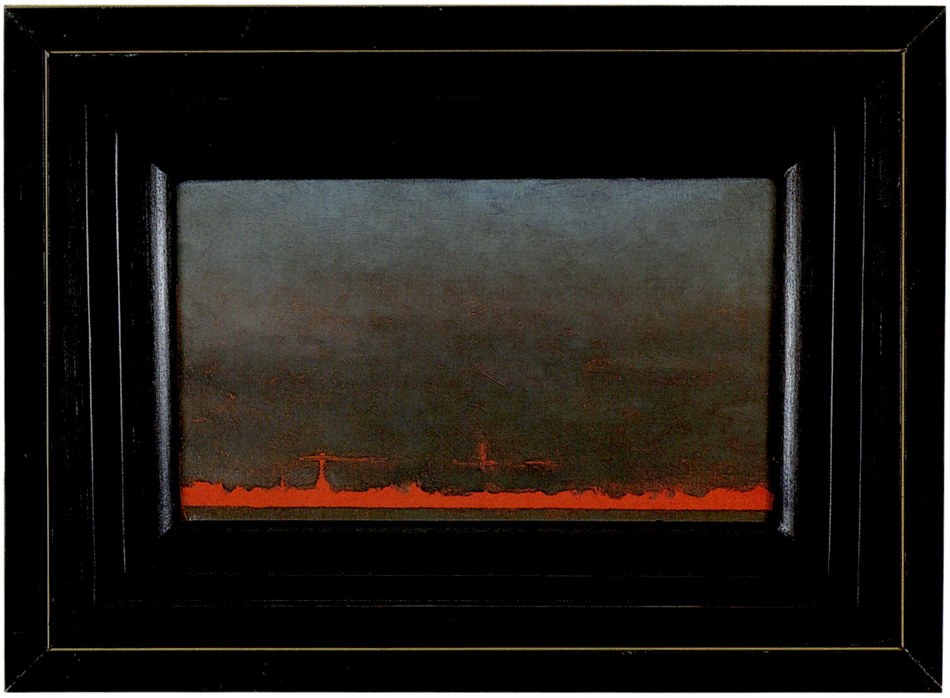

34. Mark Innerst, *View of Algiers from New Orleans*, 1985 (cat. no. 32)

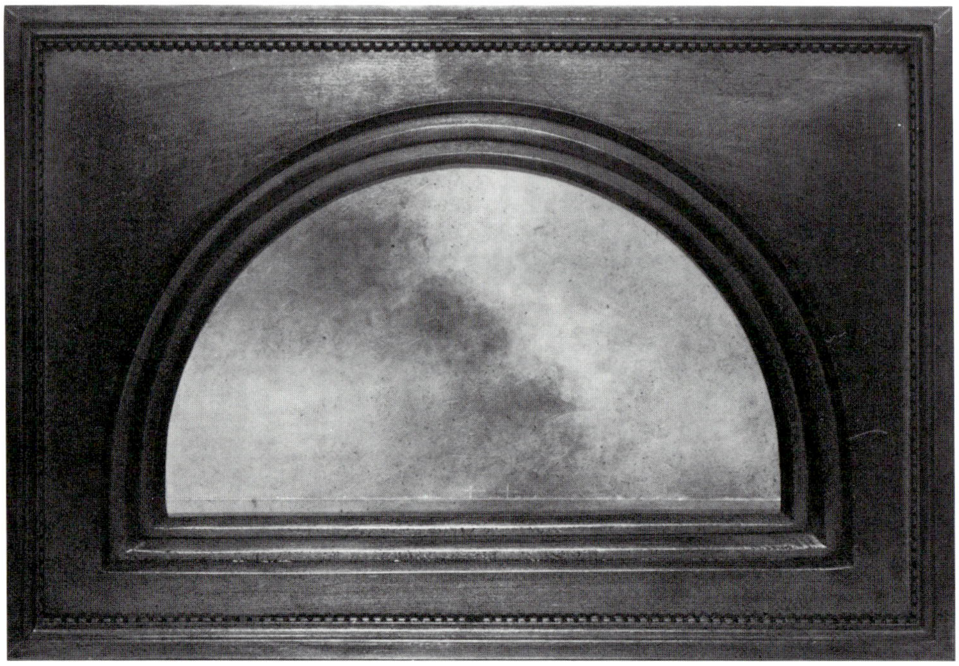

35. Mark Innerst, *Brooklyn in Flames*, 1986 (cat. no. 33)

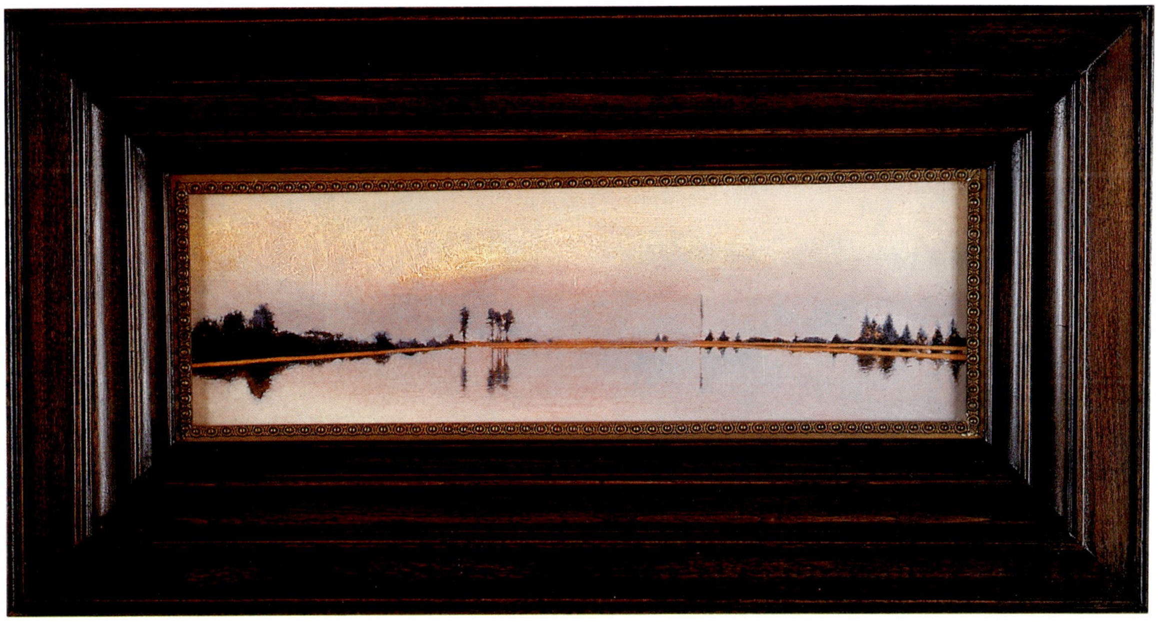

36. Mark Innerst, *Reserve*, 1987 (cat. no. 34)

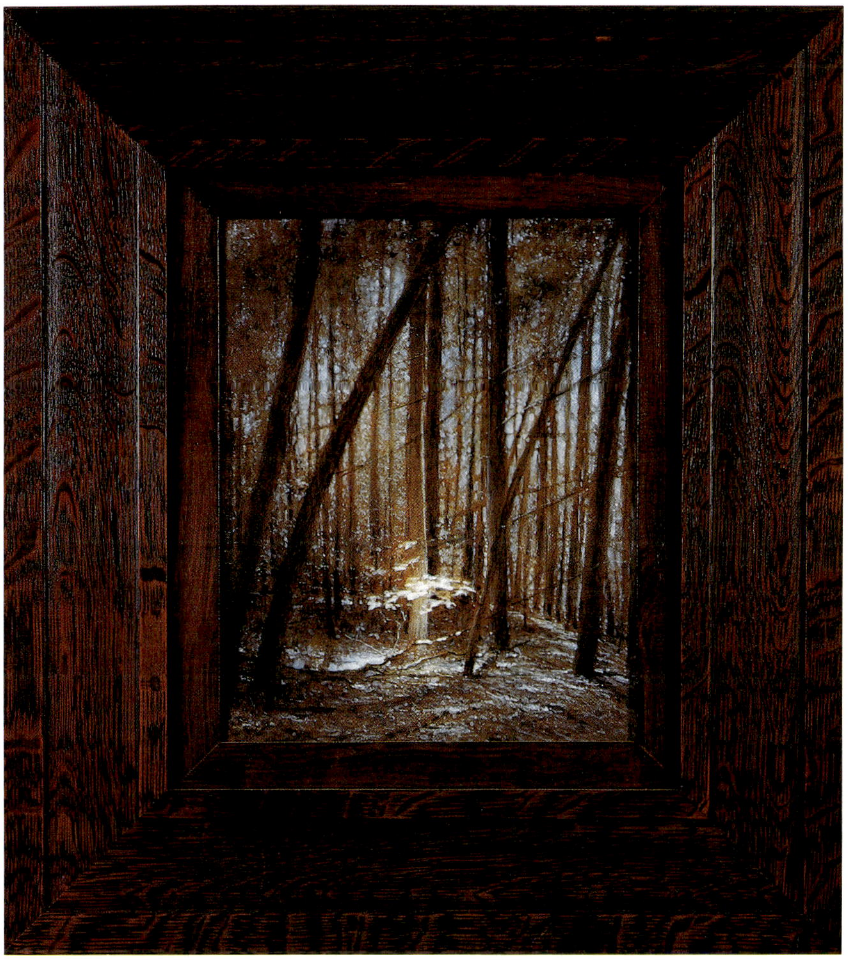

37. Mark Innerst, *In a Young Forest*, 1988 (cat. no. 35)

Neil Jenney

Neil Jenney's painterly finesse is so disarming that a viewer can find himself drawn into one of these paintings without realizing what is going on. Although the overt message of each work is pointedly spelled out in large type, the images are mysterious because they are able to evoke the true grandeur of the natural landscape while filling the viewer with genuine regret and an anxious sense of guilt for its passing.

The relative proportions of Jenney's frames and painted images are worth noting, especially since it is only in the frames that traces of the artist's personal gestures are visible. An Emersonian might interpret this as emblematic of the mass of human industry which overwhelms and encroaches upon the earth's few remaining reserves of untouched nature. Whether or not this was the artist's intention, it is impossible to ignore the somber, funereal tone that these dark, monumental frames impart to the exquisite images they enclose.

The Bruce Hardie Memorial (cat. no. 36) was named for one of the artist's childhood friends, who died just before the piece was done. The personal loss, commemorated by the initials B. H., carved into the ruined tree at the center of the image, is a metaphor for the passing of the wilderness—America's childhood friend. The stark, jagged forms of the cliff and dead branches are explained, perhaps, by the tale of *Acid Story* (cat. no. 37), which brings the evidence up very close for careful inspection. Here the frame functions as a window, with a sharp interior ledge, that surveys the desolate wood growing in suffocating proximity to the gallery wall. The sight is unbearable but compelling and filled with an aching beauty.

Jenney's epic formats and elemental themes might seem hyperbolic in another time and place. In the entertainment-oriented 1980s, however, it is difficult to attract any attention without exhibiting a great deal of drama and passion. In any case, the subject of Jenney's attention is important enough to the survival of our civilization that it merits this full-scale requiem.

Born: 1945, Torrington, Connecticut

Selected One-Person Exhibitions

1985 Carpenter & Hochman Gallery, New York
1984 Oil & Steel Gallery, Long Island City, New York
1981 University Art Museum, Berkeley, California (traveling exhibition)
1975-76 Wadsworth Atheneum, Hartford, Connecticut
1975 Blum Helman Gallery, New York
1974 Blum Helman Gallery, New York
1970 Richard Bellamy/Noah Goldowsky Gallery, New York
David Whitney Gallery, New York
1968 Gallery Rudolf Zwirner, Cologne

Selected Group Exhibitions

1987 Whitney Museum of American Art, New York, "1987 Biennial Exhibition"
1986 The Art Institute of Chicago, "Seventy-fifth American Exhibition"
1984 Whitney Museum of American Art, New York, "American Art Since 1970: Painting, Sculpture, and Drawings from the Collection of the Whitney Museum of American Art"
1982 Stedelijk Museum, Amsterdam, "'60-'80 Attitudes/Concepts/Images"
1981 Blum Helman Gallery, New York, "Bryan Hunt, Neil Jenney, Roberth Moskowitz, Donald Sultan"
1980 Blum Helman Gallery, New York, "Neil Jenney - John Tweddle"
1978-79 Whitney Museum of American Art, New York, "New Image"
1978 Blum Helman Gallery, New York, "Group Show—Nauman, Jenney, Shapiro, Serra"
The New Museum of Contemporary Art, New York, "'Bad' Painting"
1976 New York State Museum, Albany, "New York: The State of Art"
1973 Art Museum of South Texas, Corpus Christie, "Eight Artists"
1972 Kassel, West Germany, "Documenta 5"
1970 Allen Memorial Art Museum, Oberlin College, Ohio, "Three Young Americans"
1969 Finch College Museum of Art, New York, "Art in Process IV"
Whitney Museum of American Art, New York, "Anti-Illusion: Procedures/Materials"
Kunsthalle, Bern, Switzerland, "Live in Your Head: When Attitude Becomes Form (Works—Concepts—Processes—Situations—Information)"
Andrew Dickson White Museum, Cornell University, Ithaca, New York, "Earthart"
1968 Noah Goldowsky Gallery, New York
1967 Richard Bellamy/Noah Goldowsky Gallery, New York, "Arp to Artschwager: 2nd Annual Exhibition"

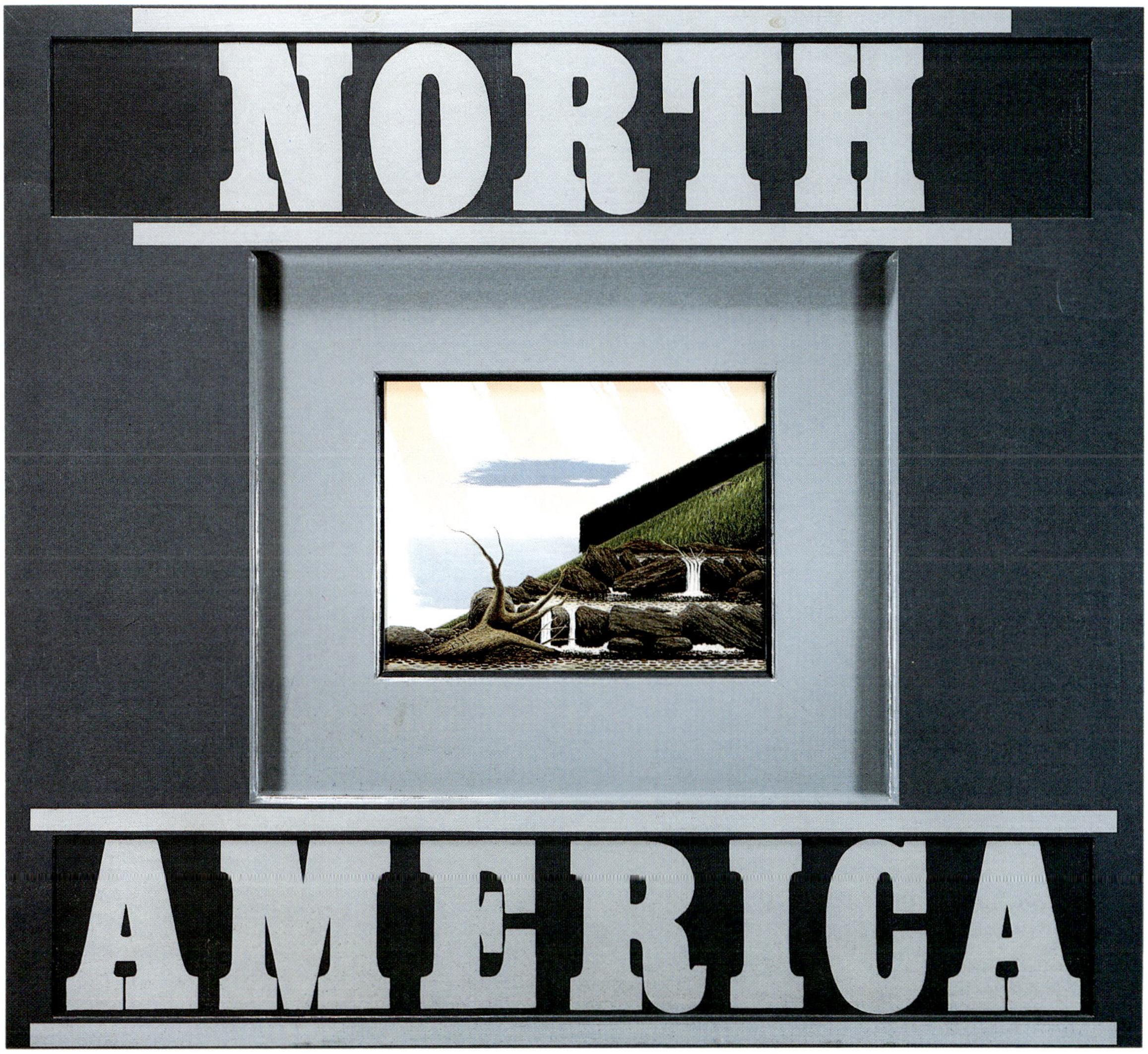

38. Neil Jenney, *The Bruce Hardie Memorial*, 1978-82 (cat. no. 36)

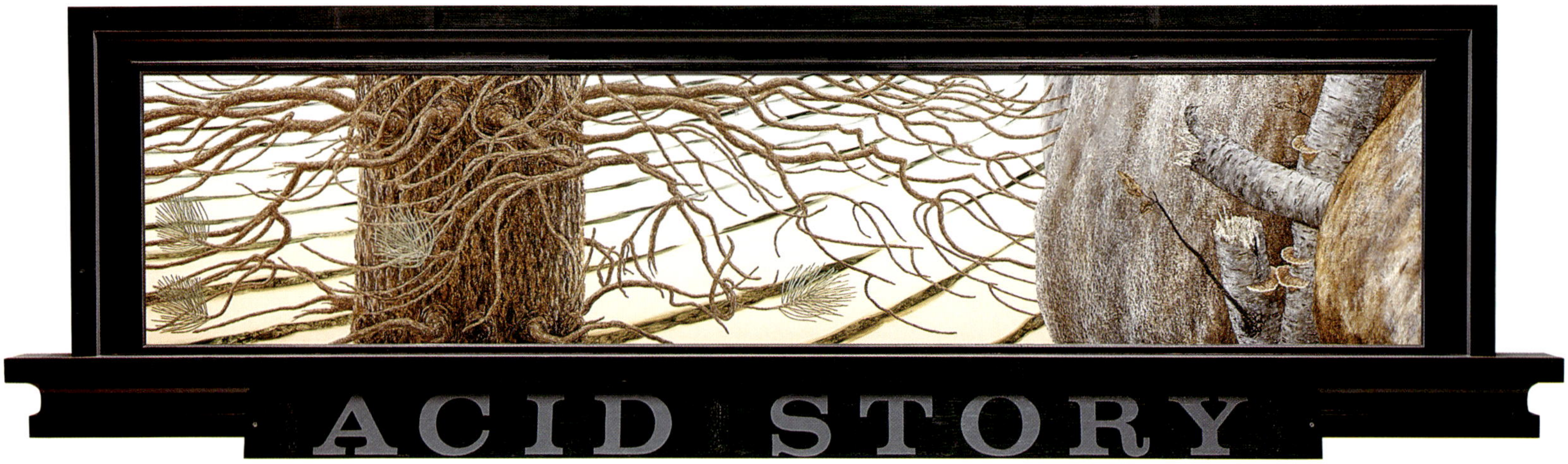

39. Neil Jenney, *Acid Story*, 1983-84 (cat. no. 37)

Alfred Leslie

Alfred Leslie's black-and-white watercolors are part of a series titled "100 Views Along the Road." Implicit in this title is a suggestion that the American landscape is often seen from a highway, which probably is the case more often than not; the wilderness Leslie depicts has the easy familiarity of a roadside scene. Since viewers know that the American continent has by now been crossed and criss-crossed countless times by roads and tracks of all descriptions, these empty views imply a land that has been laid out, used up, and deserted.

The romantic, atmospheric washes of watercolor that form Leslie's natural imagery are sharply contradicted by the harsh white rectangles that the artist inserts into his landscapes. These have been interpreted as road signs and outdoor movie screens—objects that may well have served as their initial inspiration. However, the complete lack of descriptive detail surrounding these forms gives them a more generalized, almost mythic, presence. In their precision and angularity, the rectangles refer to logic and human activity; the absence they represent replaces the inhabitants who have abandoned the landscape.

To describe these watercolors, Leslie uses the Japanese word *Notan*, which refers to a dramatic visual relationship between black and white. Within this limited palette, the artist is able to achieve a tremendous range of light effects. In *Outside Blue Water Village, New Mexico* (cat. no. 39), the light that changes from image to image conveys a sense of the passage of time, whereas in *Near Austintown Plaza, Youngstown, Ohio* (cat. no. 40), the light glowing from the horizon creates a highly specific sense of place. The light is the most naturalistic element in these paintings; it suffuses the landscape, filling the gaps left by human activity, and seems to speak of nature's regenerative power.

Born: 1927, New York

Education
1947-49 New York University
1947 The Art Students' League

Selected One-Person Exhibitions
1988 The College of St. Rose Gallery, Albany, New York, and Skidmore College Gallery, Saratoga Springs, New York, "Works on Paper"
1987 Krygier/Landau Gallery, Los Angeles
CompassRose Gallery, Chicago
Hill Gallery, Birmingham, Michigan
1986 Texas Gallery, Houston
1983-85 Oil & Steel Gallery, Long Island City, New York, "100 Views Along the Road" (traveled to Worcester Museum of Fine Arts, Massachusetts; Butler Institute of American Art, Youngstown, Ohio; Newport Harbor Art Museum, Newport Beach, California; Henry Art Gallery, Seattle, Washington; Wichita Art Museum, Kansas; Philbrook Art Center, Tulsa, Oklahoma
1983 Allan Frumkin Gallery, New York
1980 Allan Frumkin Gallery, New York
1978 Jorgensen Gallery, University of Connecticut, Storrs
Allan Frumkin Gallery, New York
1977 Allan Frumkim Gallery, Chicago
Kilcawley Center Art Gallery, Youngstown State University, Ohio
1976-77 The Museum of Fine Arts, Boston (traveled to Hirshhorn Museum and Sculpture Garden, Washington, D.C.; Museum of Contemporary Art, Chicago)
1975 Allan Frumkin Gallery, New York
1969-71 Noah Goldowsky Gallery, New York
1962 Holland Goldowsky Gallery, Chicago
Martha Jackson Gallery, New York
1961 David Anderson Gallery, New York
Martha Jackson Gallery, New York
1960 Martha Jackson Gallery, New York
1957-58 Robert Keene Gallery, Southampton, New York
1957 Tibor de Nagy Gallery, New York
1953 Tibor de Nagy Gallery, New York
1952 Tibor de Nagy Gallery, New York
1951 Tibor de Nagy Gallery, New York

Selected Group Exhibitions
Alfred Leslie has participated in hundreds of group exhibitions throughout the United States and elsewhere since the 1950s. These are far too numerous to list here.

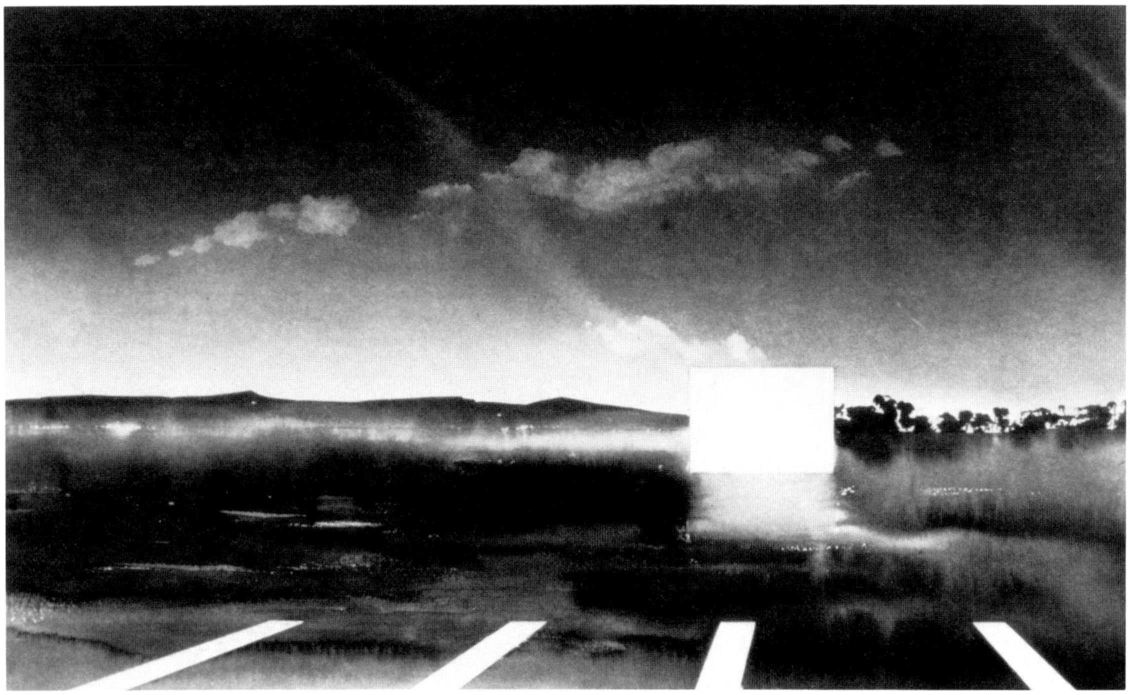

40. Alfred Leslie, *Drive-In Movie, Santa Barbara, California*, 1977-81 (cat. no. 38)

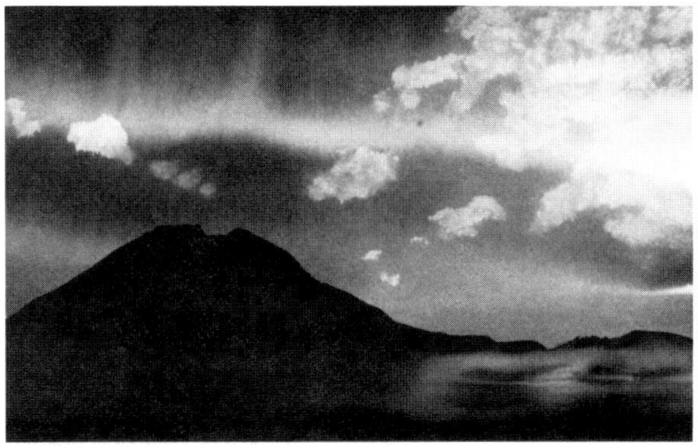

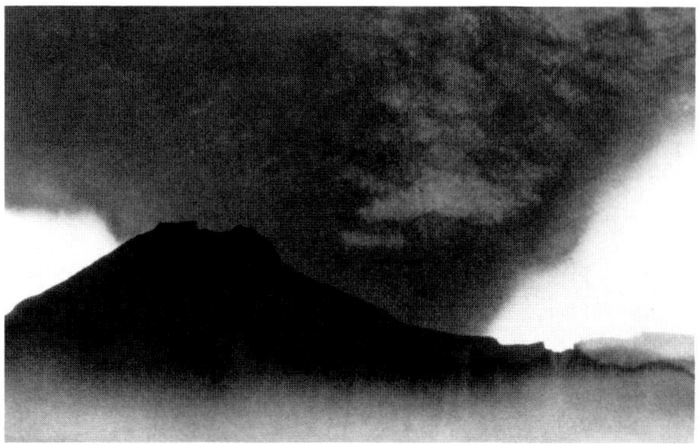

41-44. Alfred Leslie, *Outside Blue Water Village, New Mexico*, 1977-81 (cat. no. 39)

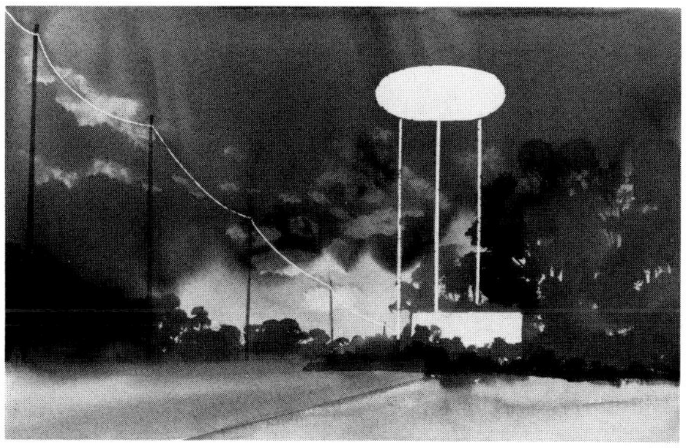

45. Alfred Leslie, *Near Austintown Plaza, Youngstown, Ohio*, 1983 (cat. no. 40)

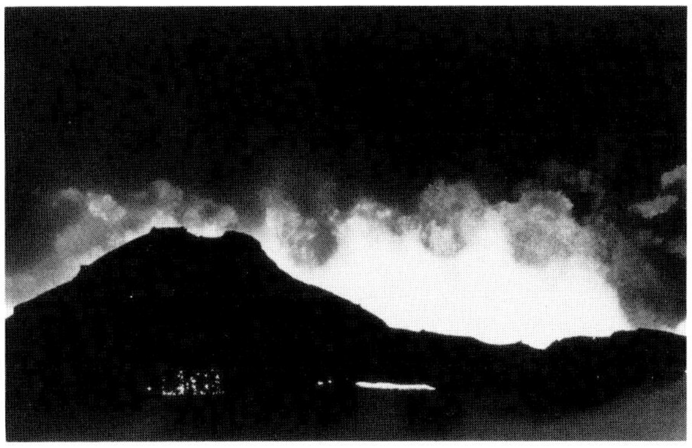

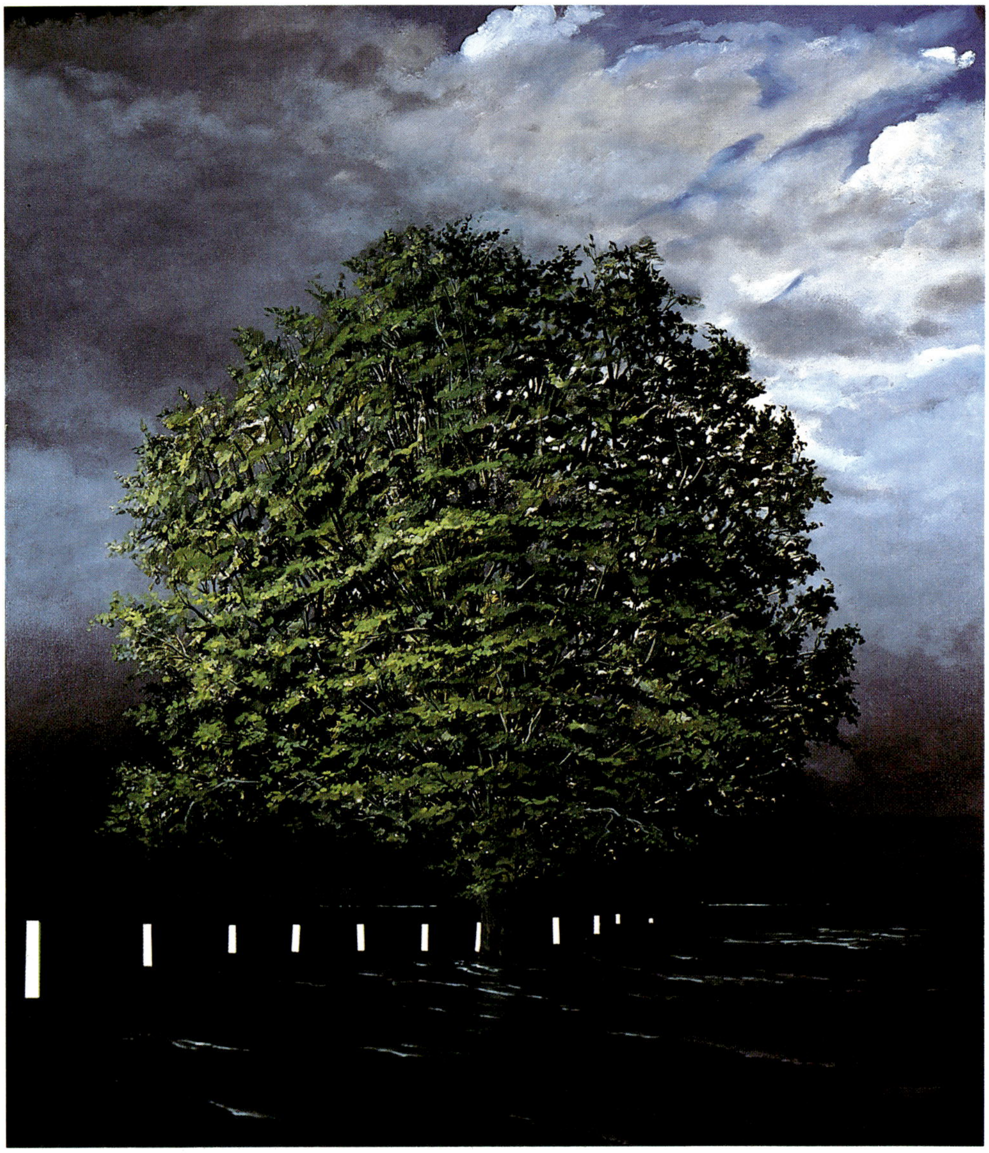

46. Alfred Leslie, *Flooded Parking Lot,* 1986 (cat. no. 41)

Robert Lobe

Robert Lobe's technique for making sculpture results in extremely specific portraits of particular natural sites. He takes large sheets of aluminum out into the woods, wraps them around selected trees and rocks, and works the surfaces with an air hammer until the metal takes on all the textural nuances of the natural bark and stone. He then cuts apart the aluminum shapes and takes them to his studio where he treats the surfaces and reconstructs the natural forms, creating sculpture that replicates most of the characteristics of its model. This process raises several interesting questions about the nature of representation.

One of the most intriguing aspects of Lobe's work is the way in which each part of the represented landscape implies a larger whole; like the mapmakers in the José Luis Borges story, the artist theoretically could make a single piece of sculpture that would represent and cover an entire forest or countryside, on a scale of one-to-one. When the information contained in a depiction is this complete, the simulation can in some ways replace the original. When Lobe's works are shown indoors, in an architectural setting, their function as a substitute for nature becomes even more apparent. The metallic forms have a far more authoritative presence than, say, a potted palm, because they present the actual scale and organic wildness of uncultivated outdoor scenes—a rare and exotic experience.

The only information that is missing is the color of the rocks and trees that served as models for these works. Richly mottled hues have been replaced with a hard, silvery monochrome which traps and reflects light in a disconcerting way. Lobe's sculpted trees have an incandescent quality—their ghostly glow seems to illuminate the other objects around them.

Born: 1945, Detroit

Education

1967 B.A., Hunter College, New York

Selected One-Person Exhibitions

1987 Anderson Gallery, Virginia Commonwealth University, Richmond
Willard Gallery, New York
1986 Willard Gallery, New York
Marian Locks Gallery, Philadelphia
1984 Willard Gallery, New York
1982 Texas Gallery, Houston
1981 Willard Gallery, New York
1980 Willard Gallery, New York
1977 Dag Hammerskjold Plaza Sculpture Garden, New York
1974 Zabriskie Gallery, New York

Selected Group Exhibitions

1988 Walker Art Center, Minneapolis, "Sculpture Inside/Outside"
1987 Blum Helman Gallery, New York, "Recent Sculpture—Joel Fisher, Mel Kendrick, Robert Lobe"
Solomon R. Guggenheim Museum, New York, "A Decade of Emerging Artists: Selections from the Exxon Series"
Massachusetts College of Art, Boston, "Tree Show"
Barbara Krakow Gallery, Boston, "The Allusive Object: Mel Kendrick, Robert Lobe, Judith Shea"
New Jersey Center for Visual Arts, Summit, "Contemporary American Landscape, Reflections of Social Change"
Whitney Museum of American Art, New York, "1987 Whitney Biennial Exhibition"
1986 P.S. I, Institute for Art and Urban Resources, Long Island City, New York, "About Place: Contemporary American Landscape"
1985 Margo Leavin Gallery, Los Angeles, "Louisa Chase—Painting, Robert Lobe—Sculpture"
1984 Margo Leavin Gallery, Los Angeles, "American Sculpture"
1983 Fay Gold Gallery, Atlanta, "Issues and Trends in Modern Art"
Solomon R. Guggenheim Museum, New York, "American Sculptors from the Permanent Collection"
The High Museum of Art, Atlanta, "Directions in Abstraction, the Uses of Nature"
1982 Gillespie-Laage-Salomon, Paris, "Trois Dimensions—Sept Americans"
The Hudson River Museum, New York, "C.A.P.S. Sculptors, 1981-2"
Freedman Gallery, Albright College, Reading, Pennsylvania, "Landscape in Sculpture"
1981 Contemporary Arts Museum, Houston, "The Americans: The Landscape"
Texas Gallery, Houston, "Selected by Donald Sultan"
1979 Willard Gallery, New York
Wave Hill, New York, "Wave Hill, the Artists View"
Albright-Knox Art Gallery, Buffalo, "Eight Sculptors"
1978 Solomon R. Guggenheim Museum, New York, "Young American Artists"
1977 Kassel, West Germany, "Dokumenta 6, Artists Books"
1976 P.S. I, Institute for Art and Urban Resources, Long Island City, New York, "A Month of Sundays"
1975 Kansas State College, Pittsburgh, "Working Drawings by Sculptors"
The Museum of Modern Art, New York, "76 Jefferson Street"
1973 Whitney Museum of American Art, New York, "Biennial Exhibition: Contemporary American Art"
1971 Whitney Museum of American Art, New York, "Recent Acquisitions"
1970 Whitney Museum of American Art, New York, "Contemporary American Sculpture"
1969 The Detroit Institute of Arts, "Other Ideas"
Whitney Museum of American Art, New York, "Anti-Illusion: Procedures/Materials"

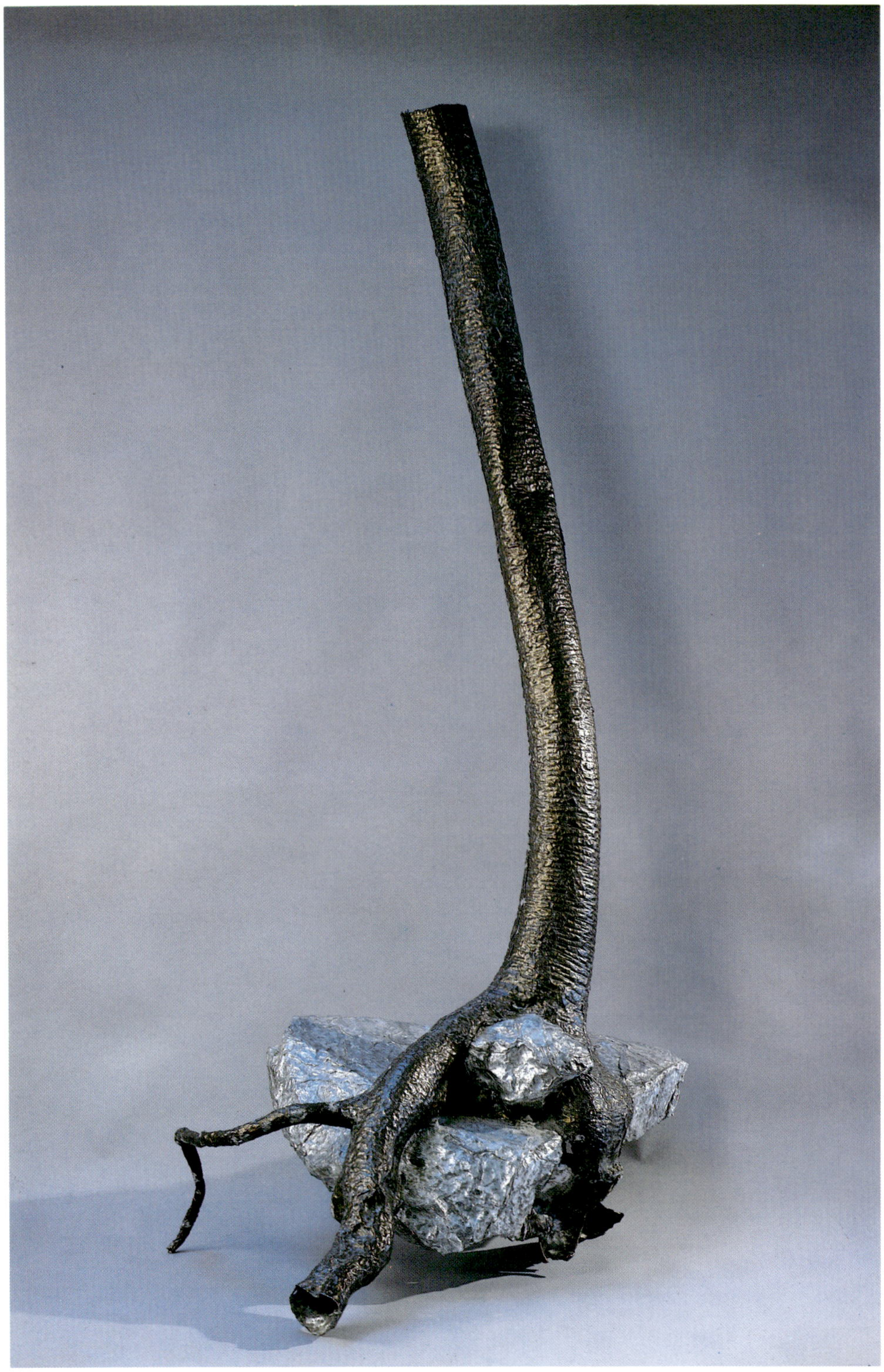

47. Robert Lobe, *Invisible Earth*, 1981 (cat. no. 42)

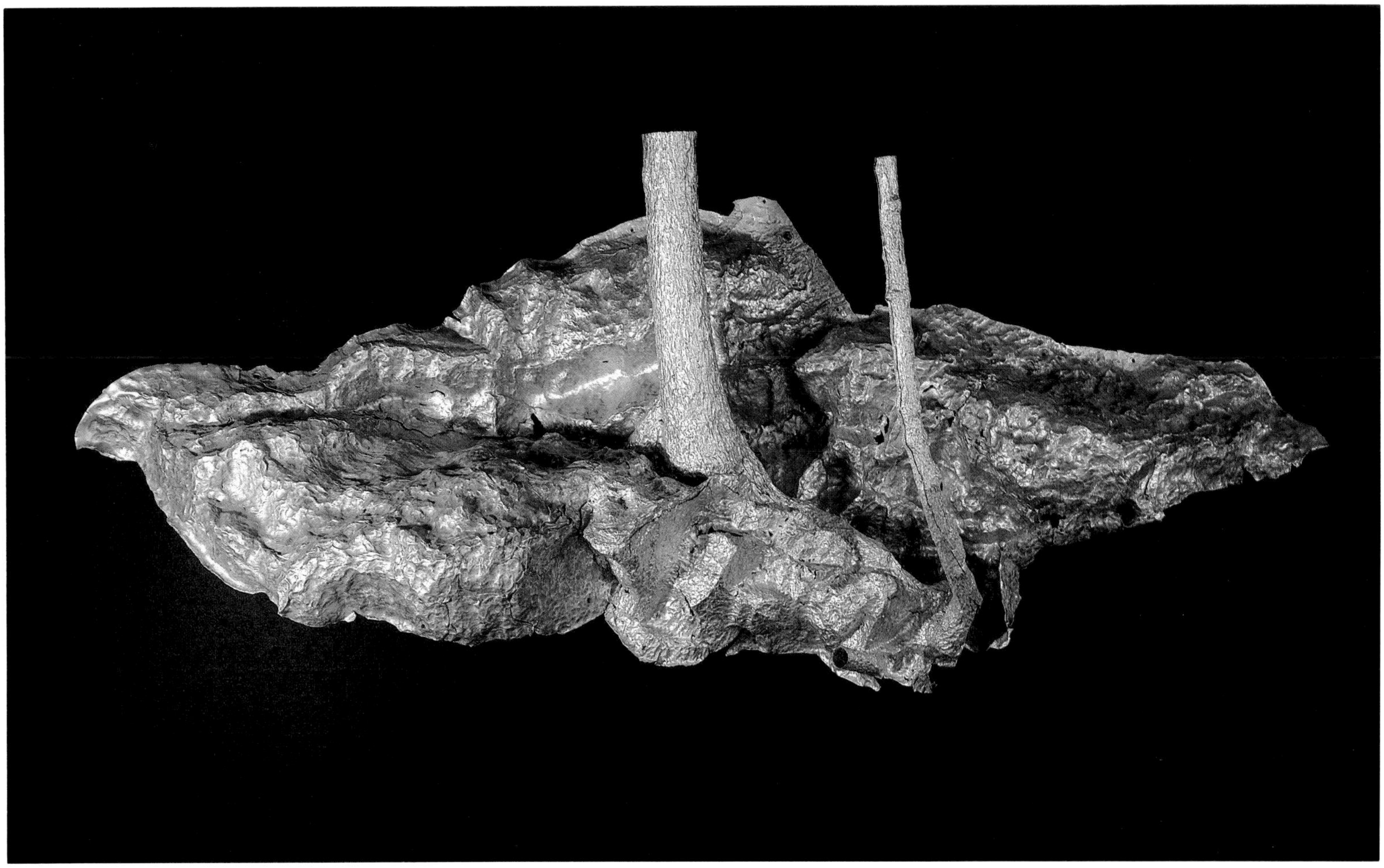

48. Robert Lobe, *Untitled C.W. #1*, 1985 (cat. no. 43)

Mary Lucier

While working on an earlier piece in which she re-created on videotape Claude Monet's garden at Giverny, Mary Lucier realized that she was exerting an enormous amount of effort in order to exclude from her work the sounds and images of traffic and industrial activity. This led her to produce *Wilderness* (cat. no. 44), in which she set out to examine the effects of civilization on the environment within the context of American traditions for representing nature.

As a starting point, Lucier turned to the nineteenth-century paintings of Thomas Cole, John F. Kensett, Fitz Hugh Lane, Sanford Gifford, and Frederic Edwin Church. While searching the Adirondacks, the Hudson River, southern Connecticut, Long Island, Cape Cod, and the coast of Maine for the landscapes that originally inspired these artists' work, she discovered how much invention and interpretation had gone into nineteenth-century representation (see Hales, pp. 15-16). While Lucier found some of the sites she was seeking in an almost untouched natural state, at others she encountered the ravages of civilization that she had been expecting to find. Thus, a ruined turn-of-the-century estate, a strip mine, and a jet stream all make appearances in *Wilderness*.

The architectural columns that support the video monitors in this piece also reflect the history and character of the relationship between nature and civilization. The foliated forms of Corinthian capitals are usually thought to have derived from the appearance of trees, a reference that is reinforced by the juxtaposition of tree trunks with Corinthian columns. These classical references evoke thoughts of the greatest human achievements, thereby framing the landscape with culture. The monitors themselves surround the natural scenes with technology, and by skillful editing, Lucier has also imposed electronic images of ornate gilt picture frames on motion shots of mountains, beaches, and icebergs, thereby bracketing her images with history and aesthetic convention. The frames that enclose the landscape on Lucier's video screens might be seen as correlatives of our relentless efforts to capture and use nature, but also to preserve its beauty in a pristine condition.

Born: 1944, Bucyrus, Ohio

Education

1965 B.A., Brandeis University, Waltham, Massachusetts

Selected One-Person Exhibitions

1987 Madison Art Center, Wisconsin, "Wintergarden"

1986 Capp Street Project, San Francisco, "Asylum (A Romance)"
University Art Museum, Berkeley, California, "Ohio at Giverny"
Video Free America, Opera Plaza Cinema, San Francisco, Retrospective multi-channel screening
Rocky Mountain Film Center, University of Colorado, Boulder, Multi-channel screening

1985 Whitney Museum of American Art at Philip Morris, New York, "Wintergarden"

1983 Museum of Art, Carnegie Institute, Pittsburgh, "Ohio at Giverny"

1981 Whitney Museum of American Art, New York, "Denman's Col (Geometry)"

1980 The Hudson River Museum, Yonkers, New York, "Planet"

1979 The Museum of Modern Art, New York, "Video Viewpoints"

1978 The Kitchen, New York, "Paris Dawn Burn" and "Lasering"

1977 And/Or, Seattle, Washington, "Untitled Display System" and "A Burn for the Bigfoot"

1976 Everson Museum of Art, Syracuse, New York, "Fire Writing"

1975 The Kitchen, New York, "Air Writing" and "Fire Writing"

Selected Group Exhibitions

1988 Museum of Art, Carnegie Institute, Pittsburgh, "American Landscape Video"

1987 Stedelijk Museum, Amsterdam, "The Arts for Television" (traveled to Museum of Contemporary Art, Los Angeles)
Walker Art Center, Minneapolis, "Viewpoints: Paul Kos, Mary Lucier"
Fundacio Caixa de Barcelona, "Biennal de Video"
Virginia Museum of Fine Arts, Richmond, "Doug Hall, Mary Lucier—Video Installations"
Kijkhuis, The Hague, "World-Wide Video Festival"

1986 Circulo de Bellas Artes, Madrid, "II Festival Nacional Video"
Artspace, Sydney, "New York City Video"

1985 The High Museum of Art, Atlanta, "Atlanta Video Festival"
Auckland City Art Gallery, New Zealand, "Monet" (traveled to Art Gallery of New South Wales, Australia; National Gallery of Victoria, Melbourne)

1984 Stedelijk Museum, Amsterdam, "The Luminous Image"
Galerie Joliet, Montreal, "Video 84"

1983 Whitney Museum of American Art, New York, "Biennial Exhibition"
The American Film Institute, Los Angeles, "National Video Festival"

1981 Espace Lyonnais d'Art Contemporain, France, "Trois Installations—Trois Visions de la Video"

1980 The American Center, Paris
Women's Interart Center, New York, "The Moving Image: Film and Video Festival"

1978 The Hudson River Museum, New York, "American Art from the '10e Biennale de Paris'"
Global Village, New York, "Women/Artists/Filmmakers"

1977 Musée d'Art Moderne, Paris, "10e Biennale de Paris"

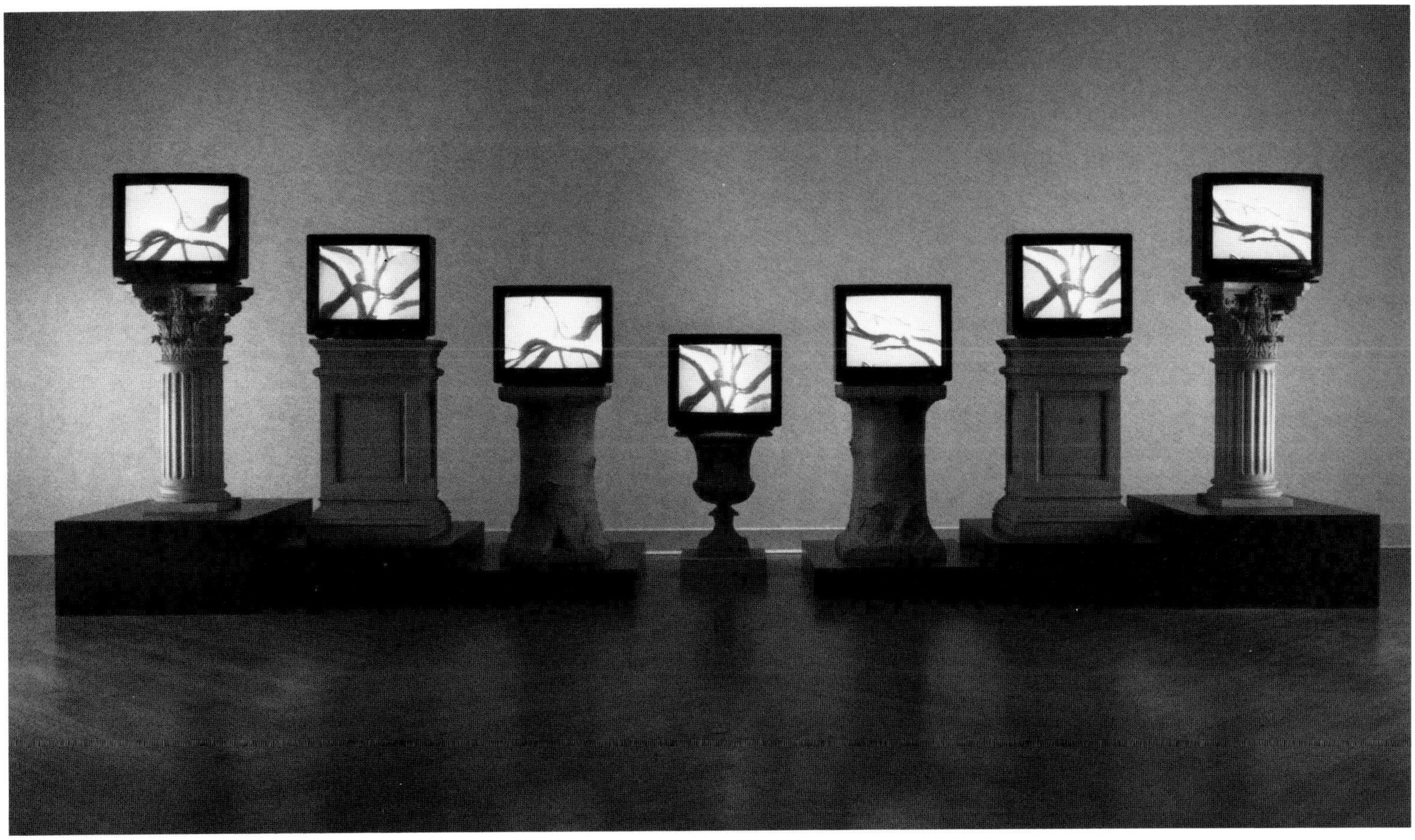

49. Mary Lucier, *Wilderness*, 1986, as installed at the Virginia Museum of Art, Richmond (cat. no. 44)

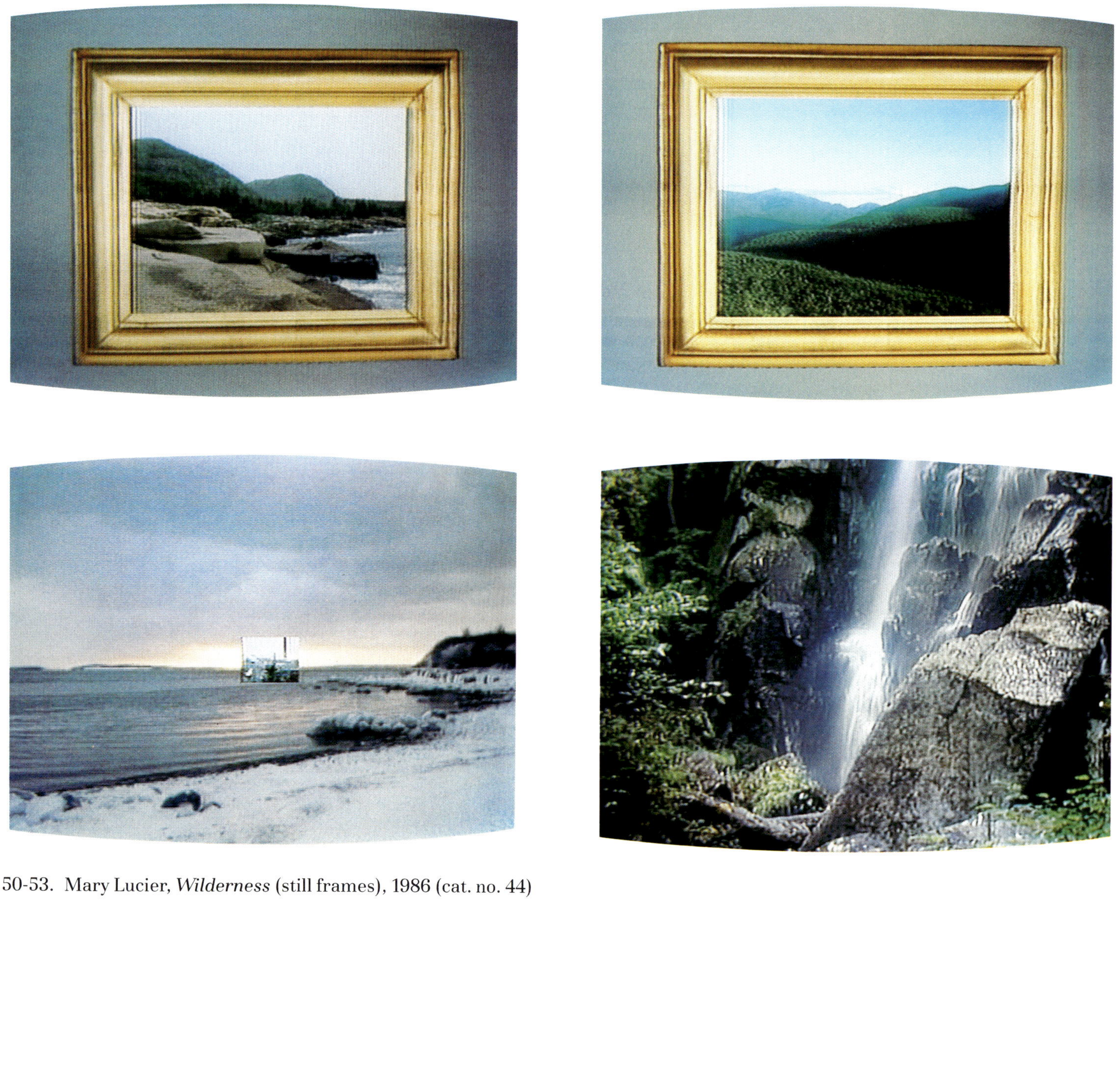

50-53. Mary Lucier, *Wilderness* (still frames), 1986 (cat. no. 44)

Michael Zwack

The humid, hazy atmosphere is as tangible as the trees in Michael Zwack's primeval forests. It obliterates all details and envelops the image in a damp, evocative mist that identifies the landscape as a memory or a dream rather than an actual place. In fact, the lush density of these unfocused scenes is virtually nonexistent today except in a few isolated areas, such as along remote reaches of the Amazon River.

The filmy effect is achieved by Zwack's unique painting technique which in itself carries a great deal of meaning. The artist crops, cuts, and juxtaposes slick commercial photographs of the landscape, then enlarges and transfers these altered images to the canvas and washes them with a layer of linseed oil, which effectively blurs their details. In other words, the subject here is not an actual plot of ground but a commodified representation; this picture of the land-as-product is then eradicated in order to restore its mystery and power.

The only clearly defined edges in these paintings and drawings are the carefully drawn borders that emphasize their separation from the viewer's space. This deliberate artifice is further reinforced by the monochromatic color which imparts an eerie glow, like the afterimage from a blinding flash of light. Primal nature, the source and origin of life, is kept at a distance and disintegrated by these effects, which conveys a sense of uneasy frustration.

Born: 1949, Buffalo

Education

1970 B.A., State University College, Buffalo

Selected One-Person Exhibitions

1987 Curt Marcus Gallery, New York
1986 Michael Kohn Gallery, Los Angeles
Weatherspoon Art Gallery, University of North Carolina, Greensboro
1985 Grace Borgenicht Gallery, New York
Nature Morte, New York
1984 Texas Gallery, Houston
1982 Metro Pictures, New York
1981 Metro Pictures, New York
1980 Studio d'Arte Cannaviello, Milan
1979 Artists Space, New York, "The Levitation of Anna"
1977 Essex Art Center, Buffalo, "Tough Bridge to Cross"
1976 Artpark, Lewiston, New York, "Artists in Residence"
1975 Hallwalls, Buffalo, "Surfacing"
1974 Gallery 219, Buffalo, "Rubberworks"

Selected Group Exhibitions

1987 Weatherspoon Art Gallery, University of North Carolina, Greensboro, "Art on Paper"
Collegiate School, New York, "Contemporary Drawings"
The Brooklyn Museum, New York, "Monumental Drawing: Works by Twenty American Artists"
1986 Curt Marcus Gallery, New York, "Inaugural Exhibition"
Diane Brown Gallery, New York, "Time After Time"
1985 Bard College, Annandale-on-Hudson, New York, "Sculpture, Procter Arts Center"
Daniel Newburg Gallery, New York, "Persona Non Gratis"
Jim Baum Gallery, Los Angeles, "Minimal Representation, Another View of New York"
1984 Museo de Arte Moderna, Rio de Janiero, "The Heroic Figure, 13 Artists from the United States" (traveled to Museo Nacional de Bellas Artes, Santiago; Museo de Arte Contemporaneo, Caracas; Contemporary Arts Museum, Houston)
Grace Borgenicht Gallery, New York, "Invitational Exhibition"
West Beach Café, Venice, California, "Landscape Revisited"
Fine Arts Center, Florida State University, Tallahassee, "Natural Genre"
Nature Morte, New York, "Civilization and the Landscape of Discontent"
The Museum of Modern Art, New York, "An International Survey of Recent Painting and Sculpture"
Indianapolis Museum of Art, Indiana, "Painting and Sculpture Today 1984"
Independent Curators, Inc., "Drawings After Photography" (traveling exhibition)
Ben Shahn Galleries, The William Patterson College of New Jersey, Wayne, "Landscapes"
1983 Semaphore Gallery, New York, "OtherViews: New Landscapes"
1982 Metro Pictures, New York
Nina Freudenheim Gallery, Buffalo, "Nineteen in New York"
Bonlow Gallery, New York, "Myth"
Herron Gallery, Indiana University, Indianapolis, "Compassionate Images (traveled to N.A.M.E. Gallery, Chicago; University of Tennessee, Knoxville)
Contemporary Arts Center, Cincinnati, Ohio, "Face It" (traveled to Allen Memorial Art Museum, Oberlin College, Ohio; College of Wooster Art Gallery, Ohio; New Gallery of Contemporary Art, Cleveland; Trisolini Gallery, Ohio University, Athens)
Middendorf Lane Gallery, Washington, D.C., "Seven from Metro Pictures"
Metro Pictures, New York
Hayden Gallery, Massachusetts Institute of Technology, Cambridge, "Great Big Drawings: Contemporary Works on Paper"
P.S. I, Institute for Art and Urban Resources, Long Island City, New York, "6 Critical Perspectives"
1981 Hartford Art School, University of Hartford, West Hartford, Connecticut, "Representation"
Metro Pictures, New York, "Drawings"
Texas Gallery, Houston, "Location"
1980 Brooke Alexander Gallery, New York, "Illustration & Allegory"
Metro Pictures, New York, "Opening Group Exhibition"
Palazzo dei Diamanti, Ferrara, Italy, "Genius Loci"
1979 World Trade Center, New York, "Site Work"
Upton Gallery, State University, College at Buffalo, "Hallwalls 5 Years" (traveled to A Space, Toronto; The New Museum, New York; The Washington Project for the Arts, Washington, D.C.)
1978 Snug Harbor Gallery, New York, "Artists by the Sea"
N.A.M.E. Gallery, Chicago, "Buffalo Chicago Exchange"
1977 Hallwalls, Buffalo, "Snow Show"
Artists Space, New York, "Silent Auction"
1976 Albright-Knox Art Gallery, Buffalo, "36th Western New York Exhibition"
Artists Committee Gallery, Buffalo, "Summer Space II"
1975 Hallwalls, Buffalo, "Working on Paper"
1974 Gallery 219, Buffalo, "Multiples"

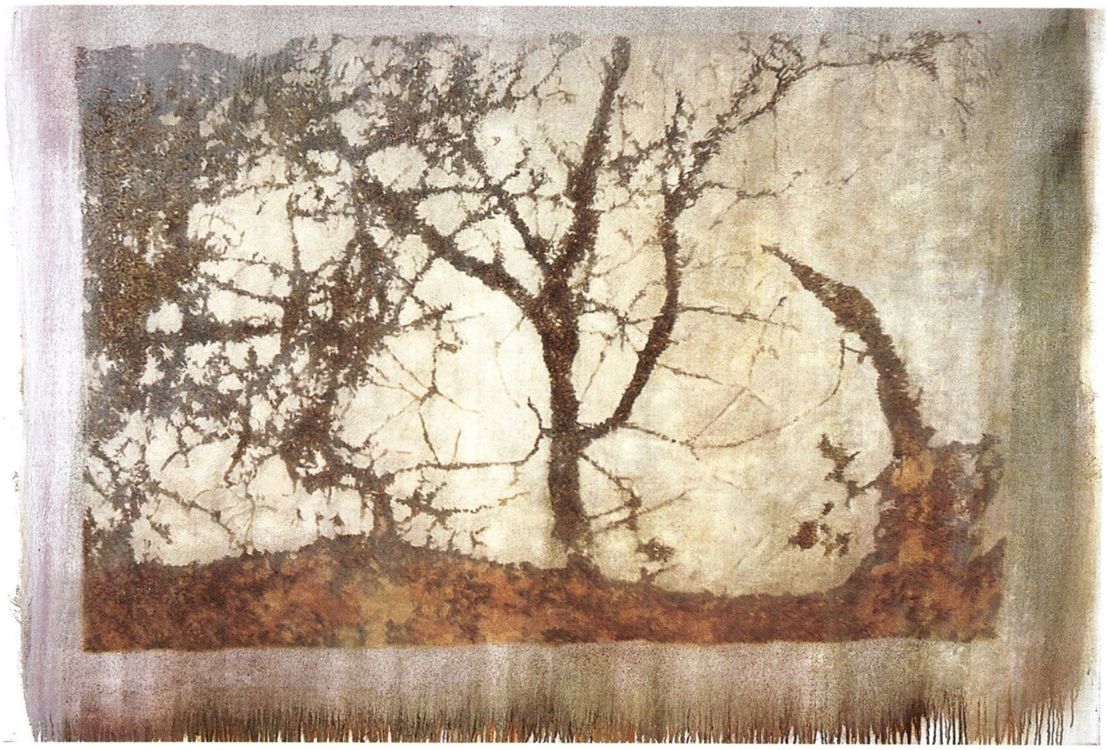

54. Michael Zwack, *History of the World*, 1985 (cat. no. 45)

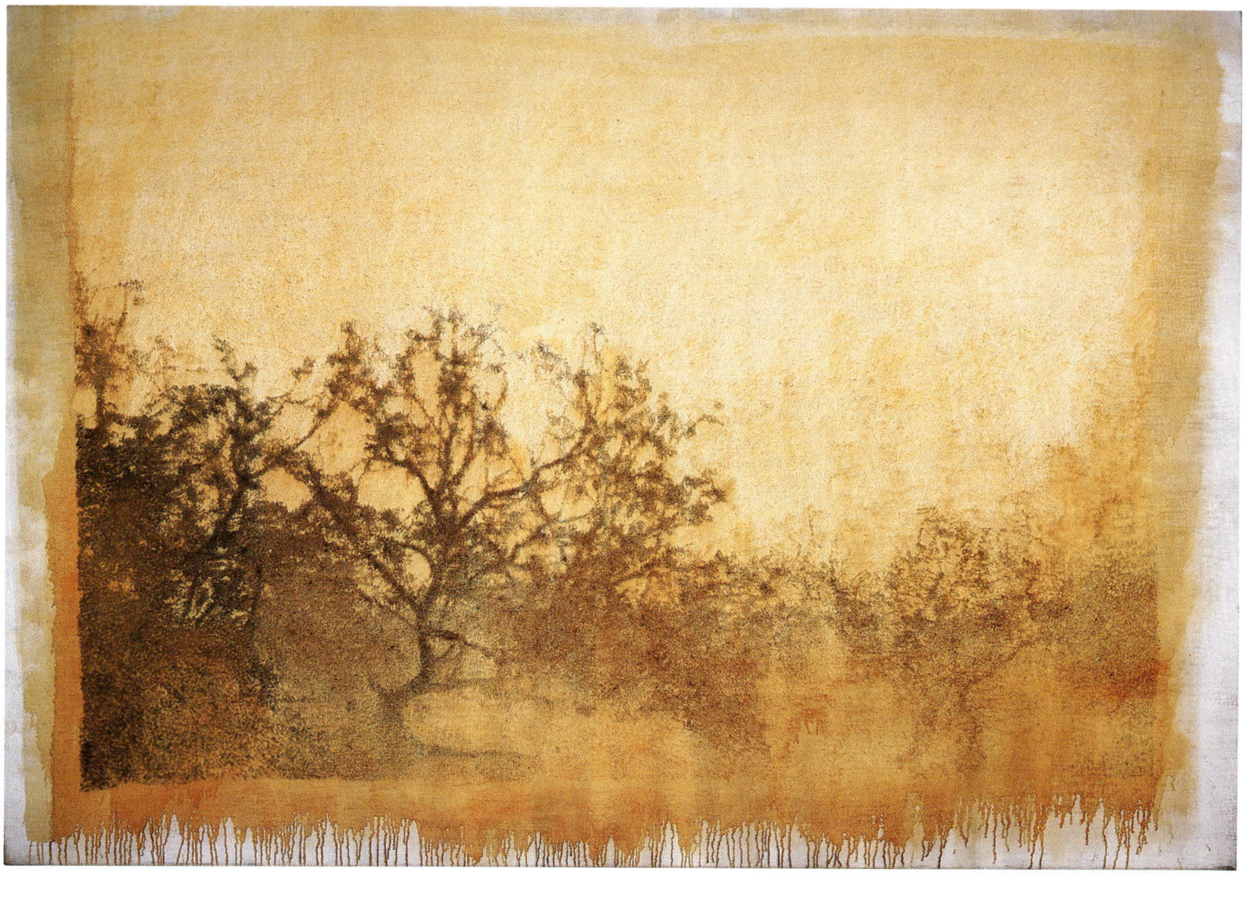

55. Michael Zwack, *History of the World*, 1986 (cat. no. 46)

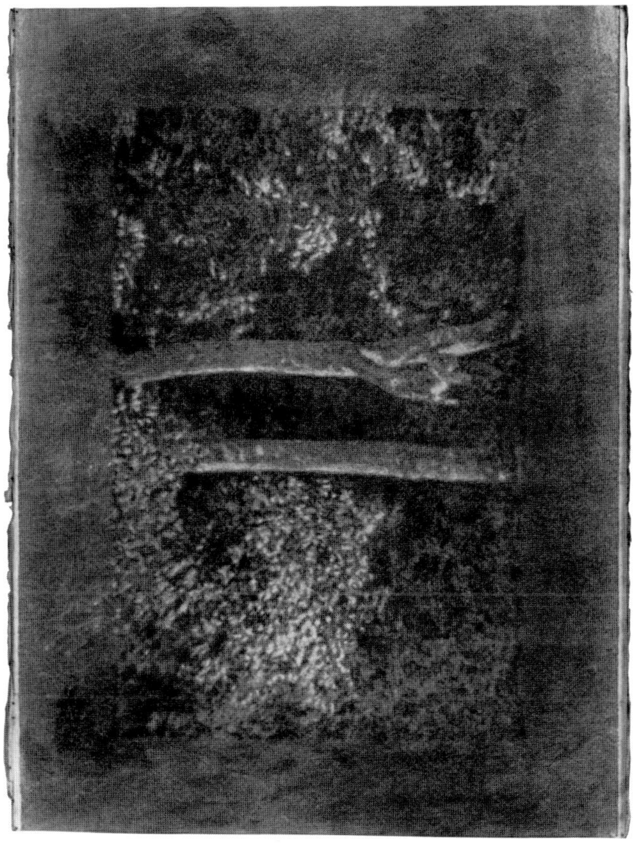

57. Michael Zwack, *History of the World*, 1987 (cat. no. 48)

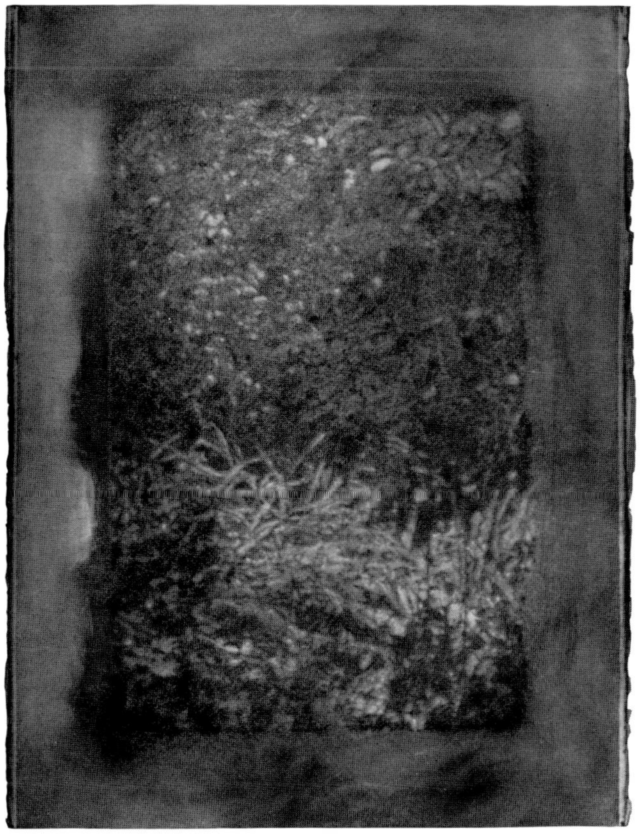

56. Michael Zwack, *History of the World*, 1987 (cat. no. 47)

Catalogue of the Exhibition

1. John Beerman, *Let Us Learn to Live Swaying*, 1986
Oil on wood and Masonite
23½ x 23½ in.
Collection Francis and John Bowes, San Francisco
Plate 1
2. John Beerman, *Quit the False Good*, 1986
Oil on Plexiglas on wood
21½ x 20½ in.
Collection John and Patricia Roche, New York
Plate 2
3. John Beerman, *Suggesting the Forgotten*, 1986
Oil on wood and Masonite
20¾ x 35½ in.
The Shearson Lehman Hutton Collection
Plate 3
4. Roger Brown, *Celebration of the Uncultivated—A Garden of the Wild*, 1980
Oil on canvas
60 x 120½ in.
The Montgomery Museum of Fine Arts, Alabama
Plate 4
5. Roger Brown, *The Black Hills*, 1984
Oil on canvas
48 x 72 in.
Collection William and Christine Robb, Winnetka, Illinois
Plate 5
6. Roger Brown, *Arctic Moon*, 1987
Oil on canvas with stuffed wolf
74½ x 49½ x 21¼ in.
Collection Mr. and Mrs. Richard Watson, New Orleans, Courtesy Arthur Roger Gallery, New Orleans
Plate 6
7. Tom Czarnopys, *Somnambulist*, 1985
Birch bark and oil paint on polyester resin
70 x 26 x 24 in.
Collection Mr. and Mrs. William J. Hokin, Chicago
Plate 7
8. Tom Czarnopys, *Birthing Figure*, 1987
Bronze with patinas
94 x 26 x 17 in.
Faye and Victor Morgenstern, Highland Park, Illinois
Plate 8
9. Tom Czarnopys, *Pietà*, 1988
Polyester resin, oil paint, elm branches, and cast plastic
110 x 52 x 47 in.
Collection Dr. and Mrs. Robert W. Stokes, Grand Rapids, Michigan
Plate 9
10. David Deutsch, *Trees on Field*, 1986
Vinyl paint on paper, mounted on aluminum
24 x 24 x 5⅛ in.
Collection Mr. and Mrs. Graham Gund, Cambridge, Massachusetts
Plate 10
11. David Deutsch, *Strike Section*, 1986-88
Gouache and flash on prepared aluminum
23½ x 11½ x 5¼ in.
Lent by the artist
Plate 11
12. David Deutsch, *Animation Regionale*, 1987
Gouache and flash on prepared aluminum
36 x 36 x 9 in.
Private Collection, Boston
Plate 12
13. Jeanne Dunning, *Untitled (bark)*, 1987
C-print and frame
18¼ x 15 x 1½ in.
Courtesy Feature, New York
Plate 13
14. Jeanne Dunning, *Untitled (branches)*, 1987
C-print and frame
13¼ x 18 x 1 in.
Courtesy Feature, New York
Plate 14
15. Jeanne Dunning, *Untitled (dead leaves)*, 1987
C-print and frame
12 x 13 x 1 in.
Courtesy Feature, New York
Plate 15
16. Jeanne Dunning, *Untitled (leaves)*, 1987
C-print and frame
14¼ x 18¾ x 1½ in.
Courtesy Feature, New York
Plate 16
17. Jeanne Dunning, *Untitled (rocks)*, 1987
C-print and frame
12¼ x 15½ x 1¼ in.
Courtesy Feature, New York
Plate 17
18. Jeanne Dunning, *Untitled (stems)*, 1987
C-print and frame
12¾ x 10¼ x 1 in.
Courtesy Feature, New York
Plate 18
19. Jeanne Dunning, *Untitled (stick)*, 1987
C-print and frame
11¾ x 16¼ x 1 in.
Courtesy Feature, New York
Plates 19, 20
20. Peter Fleps, *Untitled*, 1985
Oil on aluminum
26 x 41 x 2½ in.
Private Collection
Plate 21
21. Peter Fleps, *Land*, 1986
Oil on cinderblock and Formica laminate
37 x 22 x 11 in.
Courtesy Jack Shainman Gallery, New York
Plates 22, 23
22. Peter Fleps, *Law*, 1986
Oil on cinderblock and metal laminate
37 x 22 x 11 in.
Collection Tricia Joyce, Washington, D.C.
Plate 24
23. Peter Fleps, *One Morning*, 1986
Oil on aluminum
27 x 41 x 2½ in.
The Prudential
Plate 25
24. Peter Fleps, *Subordinate*, 1986
Oil on cinderblock and Formica laminate
37 x 22 x 11 in.
Courtesy Jack Shainman Gallery, New York
Plate 26
25. April Gornik, *Corridor*, 1984
Oil on canvas
74 x 95 in.
Collection Mr. and Mrs. Frederick Mayer, Denver, Colorado
Plate 27
26. April Gornik, *Triple Smoke*, 1986
Charcoal and pastel on paper
38 x 50 in.
Courtesy Edward Thorp Gallery, New York
Plate 28
27. April Gornik, *Biarritz*, 1987
Charcoal and dry pastel on paper
41¼ x 53¼ in.
California State University Art Museum, Long Beach
Plate 29
28. April Gornik, *The Sea at Night*, 1987
Oil on linen
80 x 84 in.
American Express Travel Related Services Company, Inc.
Plate 30
29. Robert Helm, *Spring Thaw*, 1985
Oil on wood with wood inlay
17¾ x 24¼ in.
The Equitable Life Assurance Society of the U.S.
Plate 31
30. Robert Helm, *Falling Hour*, 1986
Oil on wood with wood inlay
23¾ x 30½ in.
Neuberger Museum, State University of New York at Purchase. Museum purchase with funds made available from the Awards in the Visual Arts

Program with assistance from the Roy R. Neuberger Endowment Fund
Plate 32

31. Robert Helm, *Rain Shadow*, 1987
Oil on wood with wood inlay
23¾ x 30½ x 1½ in.
Collection Mr. and Mrs. Klaus Groenke, West Berlin
Plate 33

32. Mark Innerst, *View of Algiers from New Orleans*, 1985
Oil on acrylic on Masonite
10 x 13¾ in.
Collection Mr. and Mrs. Franklin D. Konigsberg, Los Angeles
Plate 34

33. Mark Innerst, *Brooklyn in Flames*, 1986
Oil and acrylic on board
10⅛ x 14⅞ in.
The Brooklyn Museum, New York, purchased with funds given by Harry Kahn
Plate 35

34. Mark Innerst, *Reserve*, 1987
Oil on acrylic on Masonite
12 x 21¾ in.
Collection Emily Fisher Landau, New York
Plate 36

35. Mark Innerst, *In a Young Forest*, 1988
Acrylic on board
17½ x 13 in.
Collection Robert and Honey Dootson, Bellevue, Washington, Courtesy Curt Marcus Gallery, New York
Plate 37

36. Neil Jenney, *The Bruce Hardie Memorial*, 1978-82
Oil on panel
73¼ x 80 in.
Collection Mr. and Mrs. Lewis Nerman, through the Nelson-Atkins Museum of Art, Kansas City, Missouri
Plate 38

37. Neil Jenney, *Acid Story*, 1983-84
Oil on wood
34½ x 140 x 5 in.
Collection Steve Martin, promised gift to Los Angeles County Museum of Art
Plate 39

38. Alfred Leslie, *Drive-In Movie, Santa Barbara, California*, 1977-81
Watercolor on paper
30 x 42 in.
Collection Robert Blumenthal, Chicago
Plate 40

39. Alfred Leslie, *Outside Blue Water Village, New Mexico*, 1977-81
Watercolor on paper
Suite of four, 18 x 24 in. each
Courtesy Oil & Steel Gallery, Long Island City, New York
Plates 41-44

40. Alfred Leslie, *Near Austintown Plaza, Youngstown, Ohio*, 1983
Watercolor on paper
18 x 24 in.
Courtesy Oil & Steel Gallery, Long Island City, New York
Plate 45

41. Alfred Leslie, *Flooded Parking Lot*, 1986
Oil on canvas
84 x 72 in.
Courtesy Oil & Steel Gallery, Long Island City, New York
Plate 46

42. Robert Lobe, *Invisible Earth*, 1981
Hammered aluminum
90½ x 44 x 41 in.
Collection Barry and Gail Berkus, Santa Barbara, California
Plate 47

43. Robert Lobe, *Untitled C.W. #1*, 1985
Hammered aluminum
40½ x 92 x 25¾ in.
Collection Michael Egan, Philadelphia
Plate 48

44. Mary Lucier, *Wilderness*, 1986
Video Installation
Wilderness was commissioned by the Rose Art Museum, Brandeis University, with funds from the Massachusetts Council on the Arts and Humanities New Works Program. Its national tour is being conducted by the New England Foundation for the Arts, a private, non-profit organization which develops and promotes the arts of the region. Additional funding for WILDERNESS has been provided by the National Endowment for the Arts, the New York State Council on the Arts, and the John Simon Guggenheim Memorial Foundation. This is a traveling exhibition of the New England Foundation for the Arts. Plates 49-53

45. Michael Zwack, *History of the World*, 1985
Raw pigment and oil on linen
48 x 72 in.
Courtesy Curt Marcus Gallery, New York
Plate 54

46. Michael Zwack, *History of the World*, 1986
Raw pigment and oil on canvas
60 x 86 in.
Courtesy Curt Marcus Gallery, New York
Plate 55

47. Michael Zwack, *History of the World*, 1987
Raw pigment and oil on paper
30 x 22½ in.
Courtesy Curt Marcus Gallery, New York
Plate 56

48. Michael Zwack, *History of the World*, 1987
Raw pigment and oil on paper
30 x 22½ in.
Courtesy Curt Marcus Gallery, New York
Plate 57

Photography Credits:

William H. Bengtson, Chicago, pls. 4-6
Norinne Betjemann, Philadelphia, pl. 48
Blum Helman Gallery, New York, pls. 11, 12
The Brooklyn Museum, pl. 35
Edward Cornachio, pl. 33
Frank Duffy, pls. 56, 57
The Equitable Life Assurance Society of the U.S., pl. 31
Lee Fatherree, pl. 1
Jim Frank, pl. 32
Francis Fritz, pl. 29
Los Angeles County Museum of Art, pl. 39
Mary Lucier, pls. 50-53
Wayne McCall, pl. 47
Nelson-Atkins Museum of Art, Kansas City, MO, pl. 38
Bill Orcutt, pls. 34, 36, 37, 54, 55
Stephen Petegorsky, pl. 45
Rollyn Puterbaugh, pls. 13-20
Jack Shainman Gallery, New York, pls. 22-24, 26
Rob Shelley, pl. 49
Gregory R. Staley, pl. 21
Michael Tropea, pl. 7
Tom Van Eynde, pls. 8, 9
Nicholas Walster, pl. 2
Zindman/Fremont, New York, pls. 27, 28, 30